House & Garden
A TO Z OF PLANTS

House & Garden
A TO Z OF PLANTS

chosen by
Peter Coats

Produced exclusively for ■WHSMITH

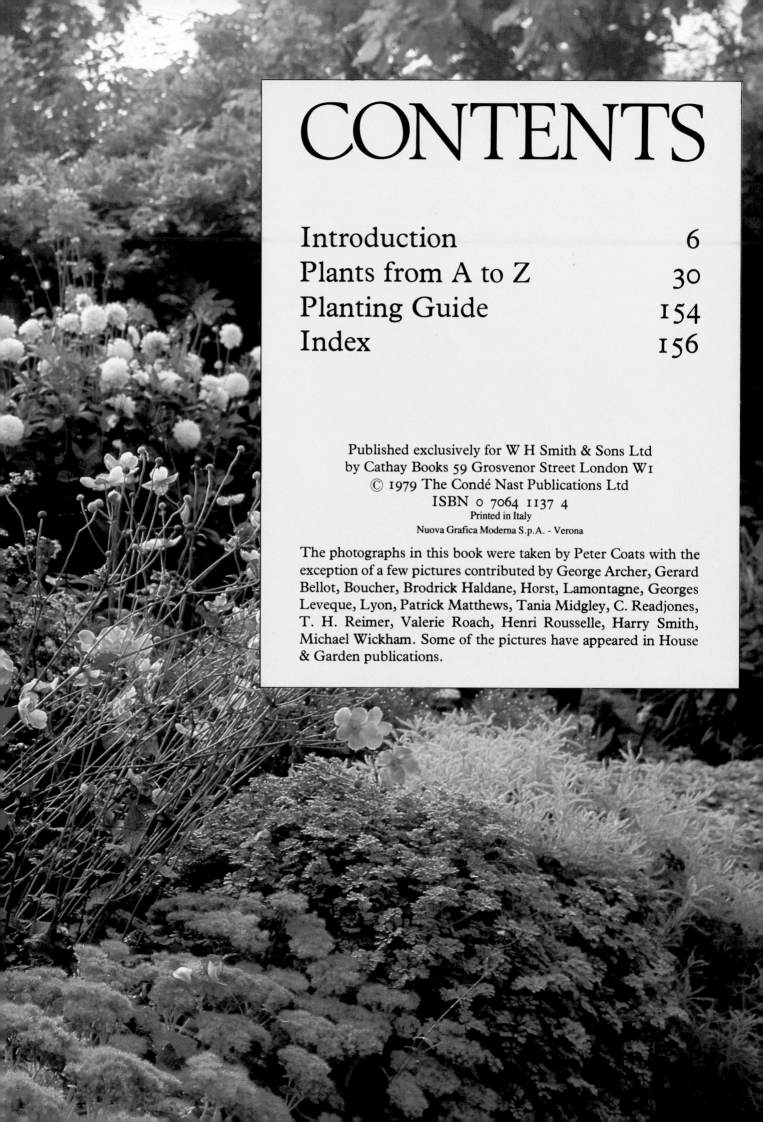

CONTENTS

Published exclusively for W H Smith & Sons Ltd
by Cathay Books 59 Grosvenor Street London W1
© 1979 The Condé Nast Publications Ltd
ISBN 0 7064 1137 4
Printed in Italy
Nuova Grafica Moderna S.p.A. - Verona

The photographs in this book were taken by Peter Coats with the exception of a few pictures contributed by George Archer, Gerard Bellot, Boucher, Brodrick Haldane, Horst, Lamontagne, Georges Leveque, Lyon, Patrick Matthews, Tania Midgley, C. Readjones, T. H. Reimer, Valerie Roach, Henri Rousselle, Harry Smith, Michael Wickham. Some of the pictures have appeared in House & Garden publications.

INTRODUCTION

Plants have been since the dawn of history a very part of our being – aesthetically, medicinally, or as food. Edible plants are not featured in this book, which introduces – from A to Z, decorative plants that, in my opinion, are the very best of their kind. A great gardener was once asked for her recipe for a successful small garden. The answer came 'of every plant family you choose, plant only the very best variety'. This has been my constant consideration while making the choice of plants shown in this book.

What do people want most in their gardens? In nine cases out of ten the answer would be 'colour'. For the garden designer and the working gardener the wish is easy to understand, but not all that easy to satisfy. The knowledgeable gardener looks for colour not only in flowers, but also in leaves, for leaves last longer than flowers. Evergreens, ever-greys, even some ever-golds bring colour and act as a screen even in the depths of winter, which can be extremely important. Moreover the permanent architecture of a garden can be created with cleverly chosen evergreens which are not always brilliantly coloured or textured in themselves, but together provide the subtle and varied 'clothing' of the garden.

There is a shrubby honeysuckle, Lonicera nitida Baggesens Gold, which glistens brightly all the year round, but comes into its own in winter when colour in the garden is rare. The golden hollies, and an Elaeagnus, pungens variegata, whose leaves seem to be splashed with gold paint, make striking, solid patches of colour in the garden.

Gardeners also look for other qualities in their selection of plants and although colour in flower or leaf is very important, variation in shapes and forms can be just as effective. A famous photographer once said that he judged a flower border by how it would look in a black and white photograph. He spoke wisely. A border composed of plants without form, such as spindly annuals and straggling shrubs, would be colourful, but lacking in dimension or any deliberate structural design which is all important once the brief flowerings are over. In the old days when gardens were bigger, balustrades, topiary, flights of steps and statues provided gardens with form. Now we rely far more on plants. Phormium tenax – the New Zealand Flax is such a plant; and if a gardener is happy enough to find the golden form – or better still – the purple – he is very

Opposite *A laburnum tunnel in the garden at Barnsley House in Gloucestershire. On either side of a paved and cobbled path leading to a sundial, grows Allium aflatunense with its spherical heads of flowers*

7

lucky. Yuccas are natives of Mexico, but for some reason condescend to thrive in northern gardens, and they, too, can give form and body to a border, and make fine exclamation marks all the year round. Acanthus, although herbaceous and therefore unimportant in winter, have been beloved by architects since the days of Greece. Euphorbias are another family of wonderfully architectural plants, newly familiar to the general gardener, and provide an impressive addition to any garden. Several varieties of euphorbia are shown in this book.

Scent is another quality that gardeners prize. Tulips, although blazing in almost every colour of the spectrum, have little scent and that is perhaps why a French philosopher condemned them as seemingly soulless, unlike lilies. But what a quantity of plants there are which can ravish our sense of smell and which for some odd reason, are not widely known. Roses, lilies and carnations leap to mind of course – but what about Daphne mezereum with its headily-scented dark red flowers that appear in early spring? Some of the less usual buddleias, such as Fallowiana alba, scent the garden for yards around and are the delight of butterflies. And the sweetest scented of all philadelphus is surely Sybille, a sprig of which, if cut, can strongly scent a whole room.

Although roses may seem to be too well-known to mention here, one can hardly write anything about scented flowers without mention of the old roses. They are, of all plants, the most sought after by the discerning gardener of today. It is only in the last fifty or so years that they have become so popular. Almost always they are referred to as 'old fashioned roses' though some – Nevada, for instance, with its creamy single flowers and rich golden stamens, only reached England in 1927; and Raubritter, with its shell-like flowers, made its first appearance in this country only three years before the War. But, however old or new, roses grown as shrubs are surely the most fashionable plants in our gardens today, and for good reason. They are easy to cultivate, need little pruning and so save labour. Their flowers have a character and, above all, a scent all their own, while some, like the Rugosas, have foliage which turns a beautiful butter yellow in the autumn.

When one thinks of old roses, two names immediately spring to mind – that of the charming Empress Josephine, and the artist Pierre Joseph Redouté. The Empress, with her extravagant but always exquisite taste, was a passionate lover of flowers and commissioned Redouté to paint all her favourite roses at Malmaison. Many of the roses immortalized in his work *Les Roses* still bloom in our gardens today, and inspire enormous enthusiasm among gardeners. Nancy Lindsay was a great gardener who loved old roses and described an exquisite species rose from China – xanthina Canary Bird – as follows: 'with its coloured

8

Opposite *In a border planted mainly with plants of golden foliage, an Onopordon arabicum, with its sharply prickled metallic leaves strikes a bold architectural note. Behind is a lilac*

stems and butter-yellow flowers, (this rose) was first observed in a Cathayan garden in about 1800 . . . a gorgeous great shrub with fee-fo-fum triangular thorns close set on cinnamon boughs with ferny leaves of jade-green hue. Their showers of dog-roses are of a lovely golden lemon, and their orbicular hips glow like rubies.'

After Miss Lindsay it is difficult to embark with confidence on the description of any rose, however much of a favourite; but I shall mention three 'old fashioned' roses which seem to have every quality: Variegata di Bologna, with its chintzy flowers of bluish-white slashed with carmine stripes, Chapeau de Napoleon, a crested Centifolia, with mossy buds and richly perfumed flowers, and the delicate Fantin Latour.

Right *Red Hot Pokers flower late and Kniphofia uvaria, H. C. Mills, shown here, is one of the most prolific*
Opposite *White delphiniums, in a richly planted border, their pale spires of flowers rising above silver leaved Artemisia palmeri*

A border in high summer has roses and lilies to scent the air, and Alchemilla mollis (Ladies Mantle) with its frothy green flowers in the foreground

12

However, it is all too easy, when lost in admiration of a beautifully planted border, or when carried away by the wonderful scents of the garden, to come back to reality with a jolt and find oneself staring at a large patch of well-established weeds. Weeds can in an alarmingly short time create havoc in a garden which a week or two before seemed a weedless Paradise. This has always been the case, but lately, in the last twenty five years or so, a new word has crept into the gardener's vocabulary – ground cover. And as gardeners grow rarer, ground cover plants have become increasingly important. For the vast majority of modern day gardeners a knowledge of ground cover plants is essential and they can be the staunchest of allies.

There are some spreading plants which are more efficient than others. Some just cover the surface of the soil with an extra layer of vegetation, a sort of leafy skin through which weeds can poke their unwelcome noses as easily as they do through bare ground. Such plants are the mossy Arenaria balearica and the grey leaved, rather attractive, but dangerously invasive Cerastium tomentosum. Far more effective are plants which rise a few inches from the surface before spreading an umbrella of leaves, thus creating an area of darkness which is totally discouraging to any plant growth other than theirs. Ideal in this respect are the herbaceous geraniums, such as G. armenum with crimson, black centred flowers, and the silky leaved G. lancastriense with flesh coloured flowers. One of the best of all ground coverers, and a beautiful plant for picking, is Alchemilla mollis. The flowers of alchemilla are arranged in heads of greenish colour, its leaves are crinkled and covered with silky hairs which hold the raindrops and sparkle after a shower.

Some shrubs can also play their part as ground coverers. Senecio greyii, one of the best of all low silver leaved shrubs is one: most of the shrubby salvias are others. Salvia atropurpurea has attractive amethyst leaves and with its low, ground-hugging habit makes an efficient blanket. Most attractive of all the salvias is the Painted Sage, with soft aromatic leaves which look as if they had been dabbed with white, pink and pale mauve paint. Genista hispanica, the Spanish Gorse, although not a very inspiring plant, forms a cushiony mass which no weed can penetrate; while any hosta – another very popular plant of today – makes a close canopy of glaucous leaves, and keeps the ground underneath as weed free as anyone could wish.

Two plants are continually mentioned under the heading of ground cover: Lamium galeobdolon and L. maculatum. Of the two L. maculatum is to be preferred, although it clings so close to the ground that stronger-growing weeds have no difficulty in getting through. L. galeobdolon on the other hand is a very overrated plant. It is not

Opposite Corner of an Irish garden owned by the distinguished American horticulturist Henry McIlhenny. The towering lilies are the strongly scented Lilium auratum, the star-rayed lily of Japan

15

particularly attractive to look at (its leaves a washed-out greenish-grey), and it is of such straggling growth that although it makes a carpet alright, it is a carpet full of holes. And once it gets a hold, it will smother everything in sight, not only weeds.

Gardens tend these days to be smaller than they used to be. Flower beds are turfed over, shrubs replace elaborate bedding out, and lawns revert to long grass. But it is still possible to have a good-looking garden: and it is all the more important to make the most of every dimension of the garden and in particular the vertical. Walls, even of the mellowest red brick or weathered stone cry out for some sort of covering. Fences or other boundaries make less attractive backgrounds and positively demand camouflage. Vertical, as opposed to horizontal gardening can

Left *Callistemon salignus from Australia, needs the shelter of a wall in all but the mildest climates. Its bottle-brush shaped flowers are remarkable for their bright yellow whiskery stamens*
Opposite *Twin borders, set with massed pinks and pansies, in the garden at Cranborne Manor in Dorset, where John Tradescant, afterwards gardener to the Stuart kings, once worked*

16

be very rewarding. But there are a few simple rules which should be followed. The soil at the base of a wall (especially a house wall) is almost always poor and dry and full of rubble which can be good for some plants – such as buddleias, but lethal to lime-haters. Climbers and wall shrubs should not be planted too near the base of the wall – planting a foot or even eighteen inches away will still enable their roots to spread outwards to find moisture. And when planting them be generous with moisture-retaining peat such as well-rotted manure and compost, to get the climbers off to a good start. And remember that walls and fences should not be smothered to such a degree that they are supporting large tangles of dry and dusty vegetation.

Roses are still one of the most popular plants for walls and some of the best roses for this purpose are the ever popular Albertine, (though its dying flowers are apt to hang on rather long,) the golden-yellow Emily Grey, which can also look very effective if trained up a tree and the pink New Dawn. Wisteria chinensis is still another excellent climbing plant, and Wisteria floribunda macrobotrys and the pink rosea are two winners. Of all the countless good clematis, the connoisseur might well choose C. armandii, montana grandiflora (particularly in its rosy-pink form, rubens) the yellow tangutica and such large flowered hybrids as Comtesse de Bouchaud, Ernest Markham, Lasurstern and the fascinating species texensis with vase shaped flowers.

There are other, less well-known wall coverers which a discerning gardener should not overlook. Hydrangea petiolaris is a most effective climber and full of character. It shows its large flat heads of white flowers, six inches or more across, in late summer and has the advantage of being self-clinging. It will do well on a north wall. For a rampant climber which, once it is established, will fast ascend the highest wall and festoon it with heart-shaped green leaves, followed by odd looking yellowish-green flowers, the Dutchman's Pipe might be chosen – Aristolochia Sipho: this is a useful climber to scramble over old tree stumps. A climber which is partially clinging and is an excellent variety for growing on a verandah or pergola, is Campsis radicans, and the variety to look for is Madame Galen. It has orange-scarlet trumpet-shaped flowers in August and September (a time when few other climbers condescend to flower), and is best cut down to the ground each spring, when strong growth will follow.

If you have a sheltered wall, warm and facing south, Fremontia californica is an attractive and rather rare wall plant. Partially evergreen, it has bright golden flowers, like buttercups, in midsummer. For those interested in the exotic, the Passion Flower is a fascinating and remarkable plant which succeeds in a warm position and sharply drained site.

Opposite Banksian roses, which only need the lightest pruning, shower over a wall in a Roman garden – Rosa banksia is only half hardy in Britain but is one of the most beautiful of roses

19

Passiflora caerulea has blue flowers that are some four inches across, while P. Constance Elliot is white. A potato might seem an odd suggestion for a wall coverer, but Solanum crispum (a close cousin of the ordinary potato) can either be grown as a bush or as a climber on a warm wall. Its deep purple flowers with their yellow centres persist from summer until early autumn. The best variety to look for is Glasnevin.

No list of climbers would be complete without an ivy or a vine. Hedera colchica variegata has large golden leaves while Hedera cristata has unusual fringed leaves. Amongst the vines, Vitis purpurea has spring leaves which start a fascinating olive colour and deepen to purple, while Vitis vinifera Brandt turns a brilliant colour in autumn, and can even produce bunches of (fairly) edible grapes.

If a garden is not walled or fenced in, it may have to be hedged, and

Left *A real plant for the connoisseur is Myosotidium nobile, the Chatham Island Forget-me-Not, with its blue heads of flowers and richly corrugated leaves. It likes a damp position and a diet of fish manure*
Opposite *Some hostas – or Plantain Lilies, have more impressive flowers than others. Here H plantaginea grandiflora complacently observes its reflection in the water*

A picture of a Kentish garden which illustrates two facets of the English garden of today – perfectly clipped yew hedges and box, and the use of groundcover in the form of blue-green leaved Hosta glauca

23

there are many hedging plants more attractive than the workaday laurel or privet. But it should be borne in mind that when you plant a new hedge, you plant once and, you hope, forever – mistakes are expensive and difficult to rectify. Hedges can be planted all through the winter, if the weather is open and the soil workable. For quick effect the laurels, quickthorn (Crataegus) and Cherry plum or myrobalan (Prunus cerasifera) make good hedges; a good hedging plant is the Chinese bush honeysuckle (Lonicera nitida) which is nowadays almost as common as privet. It dislikes light, hungry soils, unlike its lesser-known relation L. pileata yunnanensis, which will make a first-rate stout hedge. Cupressus macrocarpa is the quickest growing of all hedge plants, but has an unfortunate habit of dying off suddenly. It should not be clipped late in the season, as the young growth is liable to be killed by frost, and one should always try to buy young specimens which have been grown in pots. C. macrocarpa does particularly well when planted by the sea.

Slower growing, but with more character is a Holly (Ilex aquifolium), still the best shrub for a boundary, and fairly tolerant of town conditions. Yew (Taxus) is unrivalled, and not so slow in growing as might be supposed. Given good soil, and a dressing of bone meal every autumn, young plants two feet high – the best height to choose – should make a five foot hedge in as many years.

For something more unusual, the evergreen escallonias, macrantha and Ingramii, with pink and white flowers, do well by the sea. Griselinia littoralis is an attractive evergreen for a seaside hedge as also is Euonymus japonicus, with its shiny green or golden foliage. The deciduous Cotoneaster Simonsii, which turns scarlet in autumn, makes an effective hedge. It should be cut back every year to keep it in shape. The evergreen C. salicifolia and C. foveolata, rarely seen, are other ideal hedging plants, if clipped twice a year. A brilliantly green hedge, which is uncommon and beautiful, can be planted with the golden flowered Madeira broom (Genista virgata). It is quite hardy, and if one-year-old plants, raised in a frame, are transplanted and placed a foot apart, they will form a fine hedge in two years. Again, it needs clipping twice a year. For more ornamental hedges one might try Fuchsia Riccartonii, with its many pendant purple flowers, or F. gracilis, although these die down in autumn. R. Rugosa Blanc Double de Coubert makes a hedge as beautiful as it is protective. Other roses which can be used as hedges are R. xanthina, var. spontanea (which has butter-yellow flowers and responds to hedge training) and the hybrid musks. Several of the floribundas like the unique Iceberg, the gold flowered China Town and the subtly coloured Whisky Mac make

Opposite The unfolding croziers of waterside fern Osmunda regalis by the lake at Scotney Castle – an important Kent garden open to the public under the National Trust

25

attractive low barriers, while Atriplex halimus, a silver-grey leaved shrub, does particularly well by the sea and looks well as a wall shrub too.

Anyone whose garden has water as a feature is lucky indeed. Water can take the form of a running stream, a four acre lake, or a lily pond six feet in diameter; but however modest in extent and form, water will always add a valuable new dimension to a garden. Water lilies are almost essential for any pool. They prefer still water and as their roots like to spread out it is best to plant them in the soil that covers the whole of the bottom of the pond, rather than in baskets. Monet was the great painter of water lilies, but since his day water lilies have been immensely developed and improved. It is doubtful whether Monet ever saw the noble white Nymphaea gladstoniana – or Mrs Richmond, with her rose coloured petals which darken in shade as the flowers mature, or the bright Golden Sunrise. These are three magnificent plants, and all of comparatively recent introduction. There are many plants of differing form and colour that like to grow near or even in water, and planting the water's edge is an exciting and skilful job.

Having indulged in this introduction in a flight or two of fancy, now perhaps is the moment to stress the fact that however thoughtfully a gardener chooses his plants they will only grow well for him if he gives them good soil. Plants only give as good as they get. If you plant flowers, shrubs or trees in badly prepared soil in any garden you cannot expect them to thrive. This sounds almost too obvious a statement, but it has to be made, and made over and over again, to far too many gardeners.

What do we mean by well prepared soil? It does not just mean damp, although that is important: it means well dug, well-balanced with enough goodness in it to feed your plants' roots and, most important, it must be well-drained.

Soil varies in different parts of the country. There can be areas of different soils within a few miles of each other. Soil can be heavy or light, limey or acid, or full of chalk. Your first care on taking on a new garden – or even making a new bed, should be to recognize what kind of soil you have to deal with. Common sense will usually tell you, but if in doubt it is as well to employ a simple soil identification kit. The acid or alkaline content of soil is referred to as its pH – a reading of pH7 is neutral – a higher reading is alkaline, and a lower one is acid. The ideal pH reading is between 5·7 and 6·7.

Heavy clay soil is the most difficult soil to cope with, and is, unfortunately, the most usual soil formation to be found all over Britain. Clay soils are laborious to work, although if correctly treated they can yield fine crops. Aeration of heavy soil is very important, since it

Opposite *A rose border in the shelter of an old brick wall, edged with low cushions of golden and purple sage Salvias officinalis aurea and Purpurascens*

27

sweetens and purifies the earth and increases its fertility. In preparing heavy soil you should break it up to a depth of two to two and a half spades deep, and it is essential that the top soil should be kept on top: soil two spades down, before it is broken up, is airless, and therefore infertile. Heavy soil, when well dug, can be left to be broken up even further by the action of frost. Frost solidifies the moisture in the soil, so that when the thaw comes the earth is pulverized and is in better condition for planting. Ashes, grit and sand can be used to lighten heavy soils.

Worms should always be encouraged, as their labyrinthine tunnels act as drains. There are branded mixtures on the market which offer food for worms, which multiply accordingly. Worms are good friends to gardeners, except in lawns – but that is another story.

Light soils are altogether easier to deal with, but can present their own problems. Being porous, they dry out quickly and they benefit from being given body by the addition of peat or leaf-soil. If you are fortunate enough to be able to procure it, well-rotted stable manure is not only fertile, but highly retentive of moisture.

The ideal soil is a rich, friable loam which has been enriched and worked for years. And it is surprising in how many gardens of old cottages and converted rectories, let alone large country houses, such soil is still to be found.

Different plants, of course, do well in different soils. Some likes or dislikes are almost too well-known to mention. Rhododendrons hate lime – roses like clay. Everyone knows that, but it might be worth listing a few other plants and their preferences. Owners of gardens with acid soil are lucky in being able to grow an enormous number of desirable things – not only rhododendrons and azaleas, but maples, birches, potentillas, hypericums, lupins, ericas and almost all plants which grow from bulbs. Gardeners on chalk or limey soil will have to forget about rhododendrons and azaleas, but they still have a wide choice. Lilacs will flourish for them, as will viburnums, ceanothus, weigelas, cotoneasters, paeonies, carnations, pinks, iris, phlox, and most of the grey leaved plants such as artemisia and phlomis.

Whatever you want to grow, whether trees or shrubs or herbaceous plants, and whatever your soil, there is one quick and fairly simple way to success . . . compost. Years ago, a great expert, Maye Bruce, wrote an excellent book on compost, which was then a comparatively new word – and a new idea. The simple mysteries of compost making are outside the scope of this book; but all gardeners should master them. Compost could be called the key to successful gardening. Use compost liberally and most surely will your 'earth bring forth her increase'.

Opposite *The tunnel at Barnsley House shown on page 6 before the laburnum comes into flower. Preceding the alliums are scarlet tulips Krelage's Triumph*

Abelia (*Caprifoliaceae*) Abelia is a half hardy shrub, with attractive pink flowers, which needs a sheltered position and full sun. A. grandiflora is the strongest variety and is best planted against a wall. It flowers late.

Abutilon (*Malvaceae*) The half hardy Indian Mallow, Abutilon megapotamicum, presents rich flowers of yellow and crimson in late summer. A. vitifolium with blue flowers is hardy in a sheltered position in the south, but

it should be given some protection in winter, and pruned back after flowering.

Acacia (*Leguminosae*) The Rose Acacia has attractive pink flowers and ferny foliage. Pseudacacia (Robinia)

Opposite *Delphiniums and the flat headed flowers of Achillea Eupatorium Gold Plate. Lavender-bordered steps lead down to a garden with floribunda roses*

Below *Two plants of architectural form in one picture. To the left, Acanthus mollis, the leaves of which were the models for the Greeks when designing their Corinthian capitals – and to the right, and in sharp contrast, the imposing foliage of the New Zealand Flax, Phormium tenax*

Frisia shows leaves of golden-yellow and is a most attractive small tree. But, like all acacias, its branches are brittle.

Acaena (*Rosaceae*) The New Zealand Burr is a fascinating plant with grey and bronze ferny foliage and bright crimson seed heads in late summer. It is excellent to grow in paving, and seeds itself generously. Any good soil suits it and it will stand some shade.

Acanthus (*Acanthaceae*) Acanthus mollis and A. spinosissimus are two of the finest foliage plants for the shrub border, or in half shade. Their magnificent leaves were the inspiration of classical architects. They prefer well-drained soil and can be propagated by root cuttings.

Acer (*Aceraceae*) Of the huge family of maples these are a few of the best to grow – A. japonicum aureum, with golden leaves, A. palmatum, the Japanese Maple, A. dissectum atropurpureum, with purple leaves, A. negundo variegatum, with white variegated leaves and A. pseudoplatanus brilliantissimum, with pink young foliage in spring. Senkaki has striking young coral coloured twigs.

Achillea (*Compositae*) The achilleas all have finely modelled flower heads which give form and shape to any planting scheme. The best of the yarrows are the ever popular Gold Plate (excellent for drying), Moonshine, a pleasing pale yellow with silvery leaves, and A. ptarmica 'The Pearl', white and useful for cutting. They do not mind some lime in the soil.

Aconitum (*Ranunculaceae*) The monks-hoods offer flowers in several colours. The purple Aconitum Delavayi, the favourite blue (or white) Napellus, and the good new pale blue Sparkes Variety. A real plant for gardeners looking for something unusual is the climbing aconite, A. volubile which will grow up to eight feet on wall or pillar. They should be planted in soil which never gets too dry.

Actinidia (*Actinidiaceae*) Two actinidias are well worth garden space, but they need very different positions. Actinidia chinensis has to be placed

Opposite above *A shady path of classic paving stones is bordered on one side by a carpet of wild garlic, Allium triquetrum, an odoriferous and rampantly spreading onion, best kept to the wilder parts of the garden, though it is an efficient carpeter for a shady site*

Opposite below *Actinidia Kolomikta, unlike its relation Actinidia chinensis, is of restrained and rather slow growth, but well worth waiting for, on account of its uniquely showy leaves with their odd splashings of white and pink*

Right *Alchemilla mollis, or colloquially, Lady's Mantle, covers the ground with its umbrella shaped jade green leaves and fluffy flower heads of acid green. Alchemilla delights in a cool position and is a generous seeder in a limey soil*

Below *In a leafy corner, the white flowers of petunia are unscorched by sun, while behind, flourish the luxuriant foliage of Althaea rosea. To the right, shade tolerant Mahonia lomariifolia*

with great care, because, though extremely handsome, it is a rampant climber, and can pull down small trees with its long hairy arms. Actinidia Kolomikta, on the other hand, is of the mildest disposition, and seldom reaches a height of more than eight feet. If planted on a south wall, the three-coloured variegation (white, rose and green) of its leaves, which is the beauty of the plant, will be more developed.

Aegle (*Rutaceae*) Aegle sepiaria, in a sheltered position, will bear small orange-like fruit on its green spiny branches. Its flowers are white, and it can be used as an effective hedge.

Agapanthus (*Liliaceae*) One of the most distinguished of all tub-plants, the African Lily bears its umbels of blue flowers in July. The Headbourne Hybrids are the hardiest, and will thrive in the open ground. They were raised near Winchester and originally collected in the uplands of South Africa.

Ageratum (*Compositae*) This half hardy annual shows its powdery blue flowers from June onwards. Blue Mink is the best variety. They should be raised under glass and planted out in late May.

Ajuga (*Labiatae*) The Bugles are all good ground coverers. Ajuga reptans has flowers in spires of blue, white and rose, A. atropurpurea has purple leaves, and A. variegata leaves splashed with white. A. multicolor has foliage flushed with pink.

Alchemilla (*Rosaceae*) Alchemilla mollis is one of the best of all ground coverers with jade-green leaves and fluffy heads of greenish flowers which are the delight of flower arrangers. It is almost too generous a spreader.

Allium (*Liliaceae*) The ornamental onions can bring unique forms and some subtle colouring to the herbaceous border in late summer. A. Beesianum has pale blue flowers, flavum, hanging bells of yellow, macranthum, mauve bells in July; A. karataviense has handsome, variegated leaves. Alliums like their heads in sun and roots in shade.

Alstroemeria (*Amaryllidaceae*) The Herb Lilies offer splendid colour in summer, though some varieties, such as aurantiaca and brasiliensis, are almost too brash. The Ligtu Hybrids, however, from Peru, are subtler in shade, and excellent for cutting. All alstroemerias like full sun and well

drained sandy soil.

Althaea (*Malvaceae*) Hollyhocks are the epitome of cottage flowers. The annual Indian Spring and Indian Summer strains are of interest to lovers of simple flowers, for if sown under glass in early spring, they will flower generously in August, and in the most alluring shades of rose-pink.

Alyssum (*Cruciferae*) For dry walls or for growing in paving, few plants are brighter than the Madworts. A. saxatile citrinum with pale lemon flowers is kinder to the eye than the loud A. saxatile. Dudley Neville is a subtle biscuit colour. They should be cut back after flowering.

Amaranthus (*Amaranthaceae*) Love Lies Bleeding makes a colourful annual with its long tassels of scarlet flowers. The white form is a good looking plant

Above *Anemone japonica, unlike most anemones, flowers in late summer, and the white form is the most attractive*
Above right *Agapanthus naturalized near an Acer japonicum, with wine-red leaves. The new Headbourne Hybrid agapanthus are hardy in gardens that are not too cold*
Right *Soaring rudbeckias – pink Japanese anemone Kriemhilde, Sedum spectabile and the blue leaves of Ruta graveolens Jackman's Blue*

Opposite *Anaphalis makes a tight weed-resistant mound of silver foliage*

Above right *Artemisia Palmeri makes spires of silver leaves in summer*
Above left *Aquilegia or columbines are extremely good for the town gardens*
Left *From Japan comes the popular Anemone japonica, a plant which brings a welcome reminder of spring in early autumn. The Japanese anemones are happiest in half shade, and a cool position*

Opposite *Five kinds of Wind Flowers or anemone, the name by which Theophrastus described them more than two thousand years ago*
Top *Anemone pulsatilla – the Pasque Flower, one of the most elegant and refined in flower and leaf of any plant*
Centre left *Anemone nemorosa – the white or pale pink anemone of the woodland*
Centre right *Anemone appenina, with large blue daisy flowers*
Bottom left *A beautiful form of A. pulsatilla – A.p. rubra.*
Bottom right *A darker-blue form of Anemone blanda*

too. Both flower in late summer and are raised readily from seed. They like a place in the sun.

Amaryllis (*Amaryllidaceae*) Belladonna lilies do well in a well-drained warm position at the base of a wall. A. Belladonna is rose-coloured and sweet-smelling. The greenhouse varieties, in different colours, and sometimes striped, are known as hippeastrum. The outdoor varieties appreciate a good baking in summer.

Anaphalis (*Compositae*) Anaphalis has long lasting silvery leaves and white flowers which can be dried and made into immortelles. A. triplinervis is the variety to choose. Its compact mounds of foliage make excellent ground cover if planted in good, well-drained soil.

Anchusa (*Boraginaceae*) The borages, or alkanets, show some of the most brilliant blue flowers of summer. Morning Glory and the award winning caespitosa Loddon Royalist are two good hybrids. Opal is an attractive pale blue. Anchusa myosotidiflora, in moist soil, looks like a rather grand Forget-me-not, and does well in half shade. They can be increased by root cuttings.

Anemone (*Ranunculaceae*) The anemones, the name of which is unchanged since the days of Theophrastus (371–287 B.C.) are amongst the most beautiful of flowers for naturalizing, and some are among the earliest of spring flowers. A. appenina shows large blue daisy flowers, and likes some shade. A. blanda has flowers of deeper blue. The wild A. nemorosa makes broad clumps in moist woodland. Some forms of this, such as A. allenii, are flushed pale pink.

Anemone vulgaris, now known more usually as Anemone pulsatilla, could not be more ineptly named, as there is nothing vulgar about its appearance; in fact it is one of the most elegant and refined – both in flower and leaf, of any plant one knows. More romantically named, in English, Pasque Flower, the blue form Budapest is one of the loveliest, while the handsome rubra is a deep rosy-pink. The pulsatillas need sharp drainage.

Both pink and white forms of Japanese anemones (A. japonica) flower in late summer and are tolerant of town conditions, if given a peaty soil and moist situation. Honorine Jobert is one of the best.

Angelica (*Umbelliferae*) For fine architectural form there are few plants more rewarding than Archangelica officinalis, with its almost spherical heads of flowers and seeds. It usually dies after flowering, but generously seeds itself about. It does best in a moist situation and half shade.

Antirrhinum (*Scrophulariaceae*) There are endless varieties of snapdragons to grow from seed, or buy as young plants from the nurseryman. Two plants for the discerning gardener are A. Asarina with yellow flowers and a creeping habit, and glutinosum with creamy flowers, sticky foliage and a liking for rockwork. Some of the new strains raised from American seed are rust resistant.

Aquilegia (*Ranunculaceae*) The columbines are excellent plants for town gardens – their foliage persisting in beauty long after the flowers are past. Two for the discerning gardener are the red and white Crimson Star, and the new McKana hybrids, with large flowers in mixed colours. A. Skinneri is a rare species aquilegia from Guatamala, with yellow and orange flowers. They can be easily propagated by seed or by root division.

Arenaria (*Caryophyllaceae*) Arenaria is an excellent moss forming plant to clothe cool stonework or the base of walls. A. balearica has tiny white starry flowers, and grows well in shade.

Above left *Silver leaved plants such as the airy Artemisia Palmeri, helichrysum, and different thymes border a stone-edged path. Between the paving stones is Chrysanthemum poterium, which makes flat cushions of tiny feathery tufts of leaves that are nearly pure white*

Left *A strategically placed looking glass makes an enclosed town garden seem twice its size. Framing the 'visto' are swags of ivy, and tall plants of Arundinaria Murielae*

A. purpurascens, with pinkish flowers, prefers full sun. Any ordinary not too dry soil will suit the sandworts.

Aristolochia (*Aristolochiaceae*) Climbers with beautiful fern-like foliage, and flowers which are pipe-shaped and a brilliant orange. For warmer districts only A. Sipho is the variety to look for and the plant's colloquial name is Dutchman's Pipe. It can be increased by cuttings.

Artemisia (*Compositae*) The artemisias have several colloquial names, being known as Southern Wood, Wormwood, or, indiscriminately, Old Man and Old Woman. Their silvery foliage can be one of the beauties of the border in late summer. Some of the best are Lambrook Silver, Silver Queen, and A. versicolor, which has

Below *Astilbes and primulas make a luxuriant edging to a willow-shaded lake. Fanal is a bright red astilbe, and A. Arendsii (in the foreground) is a pleasing soft pink*

curled leaves. A. Palmeri is a fine plant but a rampant spreader. One of the few artemisias which will be happy in moist shade is the green leafed, cream flowered A. lactiflora. A. arborescens has an almost shrubby habit and feathery fronds of leaves. It likes lime.

Arum (*Araceae*) Arum Lilies, or Zantedeschia, are hardier than they were once thought, and will grow well, if planted by the waterside, or better still, actually in shallow water, where their roots are protected from frost.

Arundinaria (*Gramineae*) Bamboos grow well in town gardens, and in country ones they are useful as screens or by the waterside. Arundinaria falcata (syn Bambusa gracilis), A. Murielae and A. nitida, are three of the best to choose. They are hardy in

Left '*There are few plants more rewarding than Archangelica officinalis, with its almost spherical heads of flowers*'

Below *An informal planting of rhododendrons and azaleas with a well-placed urn beyond, to catch the eye*

all but the coldest gardens, but dislike cold winds. All bamboos benefit from a mulch in winter to protect their roots.

Aster (*Compositae*) Michaelmas Daisies, Aster novi-belgii, with their starry flowers in a dozen different shades of purple, pink, red and blue, provide a galaxy of colour at the end of summer. Some of the most attractive include Crimson Brocade, the best red yet, the purple red Gayborder Royal, pink Festival, low growing pink Jenny, and powder blue Marie Ballard. Winston Churchill has dark red flowers which are almost beetroot in colour. Michaelmas Daisies can be ruthlessly cut down to half their height in June to make stockier, thicker mounds of flower later.

Astilbe (*Saxifragaceae*) There are very few astilbes really worth garden space. But Fanal – bright crimson, the drought resisting Federsee, and pink A. Arendsii, are good plants. Most astilbes prefer to be planted in a moist situation and are colloquially known as False Goats' Beards.

Astrantia (*Umbelliferae*) The Masterworts make good border plants with their greenish flowers. A. carniolica major has spherical flowers faintly shaded with pink and is very much more spectacular than the type.

Atriplex (*Chenopodiaceae*) There are two atriplex well worth growing. A. Halimus, which makes a fine silvery leaved shrub, especially in seaside gardens, and A. hortensis, the Red Orach, a red leaved annual, and an excellent border plant if leaf colour is looked for. It associates well with plants of silver foliage.

Auricula (*Primulaceae*) Auriculas have been specialists' plants for many years and there were Auricula Societies all over the North of England and Scotland in the 18th century. Show auriculas, such as the green edged Greenfinch and the grey petalled Grey Friar, to name but two, need very special treatment and culture, but the hardier kinds, such as Golden Gleam, Gordon Douglas and Pink Lady will grow well in any open, well-drained, not too warm position. They are all plants of character and distinction.

Astilbes can be propagated by having their roots divided in winter. They prefer a not too dry position, and some shade. Deutschland, shown here, has impressive heads of white flowers in late summer

41

B

Ballota (*Labiatae*) A grey foliage plant much used in the South for bedding out schemes, but seldom used in colder climates because it is not quite hardy, and impatient of damp. It looks well in tubs or vases planted with white and pink geraniums. If grown by itself it benefits from a light clipping in August. Its original home is Crete.

Berberis (*Berberidaceae*) Of the huge family of barberrys, favourites are B. thunbergii atropurpurea, with deep claret coloured leaves, and the dwarf, B. nana. B. Wilsonae has particularly fine coral berries. Rosy Glow shows pink young foliage in spring. Barbarossa berries magnificently. B. telomaica, from Tibet, is a seldom grown, almost blue leaved, berberis, which can grow to six or seven feet. The evergreen Berberis thrive in peaty soil and the ordinary hardy kinds in any good, well dug over loam.

Bergenia (*Saxifragaceae*) Bergenia, or Saxifraga megasea, will grow almost anywhere, in shade, in tubs, and looks well planted in the front of shrub borders. They thrive in city gardens.

B. cordifolia and B. cordifolia purpurea are both good plants while the Ballawley hybrids are a great improvement on the form. For foliage fans, B. crassifolia has magnificent deeply veined round leaves, and bright pink flowers.

Bocconia (*Papaveraceae*) The Plume Poppies are imposing plants for the back of a mixed border or in groups in the shrubbery. Their glaucous green foliage has been likened to giant aces of clubs and they raise spires of cream

Opposite A border of plants chosen for contrasting foliage as well as for flower colour, at Easton Grey in Wiltshire, designed by Peter Coats. Among the plants are bergenia, red leaved Berberis nana and blue leaved Ruta graveolens Jackmans blue
Above right An imposing group of bocconia in Oslo's Botanical garden
Below right Ballota, a grey leaved plant for gardeners in climates with mild winters

Above *Bergenia cordifolia, close
planted at the base of a Japanese
lantern in a Hampshire garden. All the
bergenias are good ground coverers,
with their glossy evergreen leaves and
spreading habit. B. cordifolia has rosy
pink flowers in early spring, B.
crassifolia has particularly handsome
crinkled leaves, and the Ballawley
Hybrids have the largest crimson
flower heads*
Left *Cushions of santolina surround
the base of standard Buddleia Peace, in
an originally planned Essex garden*

Opposite *A multi-coloured head of
Decorative Kale, Brassica acephala
variegata, surely one of the most
showy vegetables of the garden*

coloured flowers in July. Also known as macleaya, they will grow in any good soil.

Boronia (*Rutaceae*) This remote relation of the rues is one of the most deliciously scented plants in the greenhouse. B. pinnata is the one to look for, but it will only be found in very special nurseries.

Brassica (*Cruciferae*) Cabbages would seem unexpected plants to recommend as border plants but the Decorative Kale, Brassica acephala variegata, with its multi-coloured leaves is a splendid plant for foliage fans.

Buddleia (*Loganiaceae*) Most of the buddleias are strongly scented and a great attraction to bees and butterflies. A few of the best are Buddleia Fallowiana, with white felted leaves and strongly fragrant mauve flowers, Buddleia caryopteridifolia with woolly leaves and sweet smelling lavender

45

flowers, Buddleia alternifolia – better as a free standing bush than against a wall, where its slender mauve sprays may be admired to the full; and several good varieties of Buddleia Davidii, such as the white Peace and pale blue Lochinch. Buddleia Colvilei is a real connoisseurs' plant, with unusually large rose coloured drooping clusters of flowers; it needs a sheltered position as it is far from hardy; but it is a very beautiful plant. All buddleias like a measure of lime in the soil.

Bupleurum (*Umbelliferae*) For some reason, this excellent shrub, with faintly glaucous leaves and yellow umbels of flowers, is not often grown though it is quite hardy; it especially thrives near the sea and stands up well to a windy position.

Above *Buddleia Davidii Peace has graceful white heads of flowers in late summer*

46

C

Caesalpinia (*Leguminoseae*) C. alpina is a real shrub for the discerning gardener, though it needs a mild climate and a sheltered position on a wall. Its canary-yellow flowers with bright red stamens, present a most exotic picture as befits a plant which is a native of the Far Orient.

Camassia (*Liliaceae*) The Quamash is a good lily-like plant for naturalizing, and the famous gardener, Miss Ellen Willmott, is said to have planted several thousand of them. C. leichtlinii, with flowers of white, purple, or blue, is the best. It is a quick increaser, and originates in North America.

Below *Campanula latifolia alba. The Great Bellflower, is, with C. Persicifolia (peach-leafed) one of the finest campanulas to grow in the wilder part of the garden. They look best in half shade and are not difficult as to soil*

Camellia (*Theaceae*) Camellias are much hardier than was once supposed, and will tolerate some lime in the soil, though they prefer this to be acid. Chief threat to camellias is early morning sunshine on the leaves after frost, so a west or north facing wall suits them best. Out of the hundreds of species and hybrid camellias listed, here are some which are of proven worth – Camellia reticulata, perhaps the best of all, C. saluenensis, C. Sasanqua, C. Williamsii (saluenensis X japonica), especially the hybrids Donation and J. C. Williams. Of the innumerable hybrids of C. japonica, Adolphe Audusson (blood-red), Comtesse Lavinia Maggi (striped white and cerise), chandleri elegans (pink flaked with white), the rose-pink, long flowering Gloire de Nantes, Lady Clare (semi-double, pink), and pure white mathotiana alba, are all first class plants.

Campanula (*Campanulaceae*) Of the taller campanulas – C. lactiflora Lod-don Anna (lilac), C. persicifolia alba (white), C. persicifolia Telham Beauty (single blue), and Pouffe, a lower growing cushiony variety, with cup shaped mauve flowers are the best. Of the innumerable smaller varieties C. carpatica Blue Moon-Light, C. carpatica White Star, C. muralis major, C. pilosa superba, flowering in May, and C. warleyensis, flowering in August, are all good plants for paving or rock work. The last named was raised in the famous Essex garden of Miss Ellen Willmott.

Campsis (*Bignoniaceae*) These are showy climbers for a sheltered wall, with pinnate leaves and pendant orange trumpet flowers. C. chinensis, Madame Galen, is hardier than most. They should be pruned hard back in early spring, and strong growth will follow.

Carpenteria (*Saxifragaceae*) Carpenterias are handsome white flowered shrubs to grow against a wall; but they are apt to be short lived. The best form to plant is Ladham's Variety; once planted, it should never be disturbed. The flowers are white with beautiful golden stamens. Carpenteria needs a light warm soil.

Caryopteris (*Verbenaceae*) Caryopteris clandonensis is the best hybrid, and is quite hardy in a well-drained sunny position: it has lanceolate leaves and flowers of electric blue in autumn. C. tangutica is even hardier.

All caryopteris should be pruned back in spring and they do not mind a lime soil.

Catananche (*Compositae*) The herbaceous C. caerulea is the best form of catananche and shows crisp blue papery flowers in June. The ancient Greeks used catananche in love-potions. It grows well in any good soil and comes easily from seed.

Ceanothus (*Rhamnaceae*) For blue flowering shrubs ceanothus take the prize. They are lime tolerant and good plants for seaside gardens. Six of the very best are the evergreen Autumnal

Blue, and the rich blue Delight, the dark blue densely-growing dentatus, thyrsiflorus and the unusual rosy-pink Perle Rose. Topaz is a richer blue than the commoner summer-flowering Gloire de Versailles. Ceanothus are also known as Californian Lilacs.

Celmisia (*Compositae*) The celmisias originated in New Zealand and make attractive plants for the well-drained border or rock-garden. C. argentea and C. ramulosa are very special plants, as is the large flowered C. Hookeri. Celmisias prefer a peaty acid soil, and some protection in winter.

Ceratostigma (*Plumbaginaceae*) One of the best of all small shrubs for

Left *Cerastium tomentosum, 'Snow-in-Summer' makes an effective plant in paving, but can be too invasive, and once planted, is difficult to eradicate*
Opposite *A group of finely contrasting foliage with a mass of Cineraria maritima in the foreground, and the sword-like leaves of Yucca gloriosa above*
Below *Caltha palustris – the old-fashioned Marsh Marigold, is still one of the most spectacular plants for the waterside. Alba is a single white form, while C. flore pleno has double flowers*

colour in late summer, ceratostigma bears its blue flowers over a long period from July onwards. Its brown seed heads are attractive too. Although quite hardy, it is a plant which usually dies down to the ground in winter – but quickly grows again in spring. Often, and confusingly, known as Plumbago.

Chionodoxa (*Liliaceae*) There are several lesser known species chionodoxas which are quite as attractive as the well known blue Glory of the Snow. C. Luciliae rosea is pink; C. cretica is blue and white; while the seldom grown C. grandiflora is mauve. All Chionodoxas will spread freely.

Choisya (*Rutaceae*) Choisya ternata. The Mexican Orange Blossom, is a most attractive evergreen shrub with spicy leaves and cream-white flowers. It is only really happy against a wall as it does not like being blown about. It strikes easily from cuttings.

Cimicifuga (*Ranunculaceae*) Cimicifuga succeeds well in shade and its slender spires of white flowers can light up a dark corner of the shrubbery. A rather moist soil suits it best. It can be increased by the means of root cuttings in spring.

Cineraria maritima (*Compositae*) This has handsome deeply cut leaves which are almost white. It flourishes by the sea, and in poor soil and full sunlight. It is hardy only in the mildest climates and is best raised every year from cuttings. Its yellow daisy flowers are undistinguished and better snipped off. It is known colloquially as Dusty Miller.

Cistus (*Cistaceae*) Cistus delight in poor soil and full sun. They thrive on chalk, but resent disturbance. C. corbariensis is perhaps the hardiest: it has white flowers and fresh green leaves. C. cyprius, with white flowers marked with crimson, can grow to a height of nine feet. C. pulverulentus Sunset is one of the most attractive of all cistus, with silvery leaves and

Above *Clematis montana, whether in its usual white form or the less common Clematis montana Pink Perfection is one of the glories of early summer. Clematis montana is so robust that it has been described as the ideal covering for 'Twentieth century eye-sores – such as garages'*

Above left *Clematis Durandii has a semi-herbaceous habit*

Centre *The popular Clematis Jackmannii catches the sun*

Below *One of the best of all clematis in late summer is the rosy purple Victoria*

pink flowers, as has the most beautiful hybrid Silver Pink. C. algarvensis makes a neat low shrub covered with yellow flowers. All the last three are good plants for paving.

Clematis (*Ranunculaceae*) The large flowered clematis are among the most beautiful of climbers – and they thrive with their flowers in the sun, and their roots in the shade. The north side of a low wall facing south, is their ideal position. Out of the hundreds available, a list of a few very special plants might include Belle of Woking, with silvery mauve flowers that are sometimes almost green, the rose-coloured Comtesse de Bouchard, the wine-red Ernest Markham, deep purple Victoria, semi-herbaceous Durandii, cream-white Henryi, sun-loving white Huldine, white Madame Boisselot, favourite Lasurstern, pale blue Mrs Cholmondely, and deep purple The President.

Species or smaller flowered clematis have their own fascination, and are sometimes easier to grow than the showier hybrids. All very desirable plants are the Francis Rivis form of C. alpina, C. Armandii and C. chrysocoma. The winter flowering C. calycina, the pink forms of C. montana, Pink Perfection or rubens, C. Rehderiana with flowers of pale primrose in autumn – the yellow C. tangutica, not only for its flowers but for its feathery seed pods, too: the rather rare C. texensis with small vase-shaped scarlet flowers, and the pink flowered, vigorous C. vedrariensis rosea. For the border there are attractive herbaceous clematis such as C. heracleifolia.

Clianthus (*Leguminosae*) The Lobster Claw plant has the most exotic appearance but will only succeed, in the open air, in the most sheltered position and in sharply drained soil. Its flowers are bright red. There is a less arresting, but rarer, white form – Clianthus puniceus albus. It can be grown as a pot plant in the greenhouse and placed outside against a wall in early summer.

Cobaea scandens (*Polemoniaceae*) One of the fastest of all climbers – cobaea is not hardy in Northern gardens, but can be readily raised from seed and planted out, when it will shoot up to a height of eight or nine feet in no time. Its bells are greenish-purple, and will last well if cut. The white form is less attractive.

Colchicum (*Liliaceae*) The Autumn Crocus have a strange, slightly sinister, charm of their own. They belong to the lily family – unlike ordinary crocuses, which are iridaceae. There are many good new hybrids, such as the violet Autumn Queen, Violet Queen, and the large flowered Water-Lily. They should be planted somewhere where their rather coarse spring foliage is not in the way.

Convolvulus (*Convolvulaceae*) Of the many convulvulus there are three which are well worth growing. The low shrubby C. Cneorum – with grey leaves and white flowers flushed with pink, and two annual convolvulus, the well known blue C. major Morning Glory and C. minor Crimson Monarch.

Above right Clematis montana is one of the most generous of spring flowers and will quickly curtain any wall. In the back ground and appreciative of its sheltered position, Ceanothus impressus

Opposite Clematis, ideal plants for walls or fences, prefer to have their roots in shade, their flowers in full sun. The large flowered varieties are particularly decorative, such as the white Marie Boisselot shown here. Another good white clematis, with a darker centre, is henryi

Cornus (*Cornaceae*) There are many Dogwoods, some of the easiest culture, some more difficult. For the connoisseurs there are C. florida, the American Dogwood, which seldom flowers as well in Britain as it does in America. Apple Blossom and Cherokee Chief are good ones to look for; C. Kousa, from Japan, with cream-white flowers, tinged with rose, borne along its horizontally growing branches in May, colours well in autumn; Cornus Mas is the yellow flowered, red berried Cornelian Cherry, and C. nuttallii is a vigorous grower with white flowers touched with pink. Easier plants, but first class doers, are the well known C. alternifolia argentea, with variegated leaves; C. sibirica, with sealing wax red stems, if cut down yearly; and C. stolonifera flaviramea, with yellow stems. The last two Dogwoods thrive in damp.

Cortaderia (*Gramineae*) Several of the Pampas Grasses can provide handsome outlines for the garden in late summer. Cortaderia argentea is the usual silver headed form. C. carnea has plumes tinted with pink, while C. compacta is a miniature Pampas Grass which could find a place in the smallest garden. All Pampas Grass can be increased by division in April. A deep well drained loamy soil is what they prefer.

Cotoneaster (*Rosaceae*) Cotoneasters are the most easy going of shrubs and will succeed in almost any soil or situation. Some are prostrate in form – others make elegant trees; most berry and colour brightly in autumn.

A few for the discerning gardener are C. Aldenhamensis, C. bullata macrophylla, C. conspicua decora, with particularly bright berries, the ground-hugging C. Dammeri, the brilliant autumn colouring C. disticha tongolensis; the variegated form of the popular C. horizontalis, and the easily trained hybridus pendulus.

Crambe (*Cruciferae*) This is one of the great border and shrubbery plants – making four foot high rosettes of vast cabbage leaves, surmounted by a cloud of white flowers in July. The variety Kotschyana is said to have particularly large flowers (RHS Dictionary). The Crambes originate in the Caucasus.

Crinum (*Amaryllidaceae*) The Cape Lilies are handsome late summer flowering plants for a warm position and in well-drained soil, such as the foot of a wall. C. powelli has rose-pink trumpet flowers. C. p. album is white. C. p. Krelagei has extra large pale rose flowers. Once planted in the right place, they should not be disturbed.

Crocus (*Iridaceae*) Crocuses are the ideal plants for naturalizing – indeed, unless they are grown in pots, they can hardly be grown in any other way. Some of the species crocuses are particularly attractive. A few for the discerning gardener would include the sweet smelling Scotch Crocus, Crocus biflorus, cream marked with purple; the orange chrysanthus; the lilac thomasinianus, and the large flowered white or purple vernus. Of the many beautiful seedlings and hybrids raised from these, Crocus biflorus weldenii Fairy, chrysanthus Blue Pearl, and deep orange chrysanthus E. A. Bowles, and the unusual, almost dark blue, C. vernus Naval Guard are quite outstanding. All crocus like to grow in full sun.

Cyclamen (*Primulaceae*) The hardy cyclamen can provide flowers as well as the most delightful marbled foliage, for many months of the year. C. atkinsii flowers through January to March, C. repandum and C. coum from March till April, C. europaeum from August to October, as does the popular C. neapolitanum. The rough grass under a large tree is a good place to plant them.

Cydonia (*Rosaceae*) Chaenomeles is the beloved 'japonica' of one's childhood, and has suffered several changes of name in the last twenty years, having been known as Pyrus japonica, chaenomeles, and cydonia. The best of the flowering quinces are C. lagenaria Brilliant (bright red), nivalis (white), and the best of all, Knaphill Scarlet. C. moerloesii has flowers like appleblossom. Side shoots can be shortened after flowering.

Cynara (*Compositae*) The artichokes, with their sculptured silver leaves, can contribute magnificent form to the mixed border. The Cardoon, C. Cardunculus is the most imposing. They will only give of their best if planted in deeply dug and well prepared soil.

Cytisus (*Leguminosae*) C. Battandieri, the Moroccan Broom, is a shrub with silvery leaves and cone shaped flower heads, which some think smell of pineapples, and some of quince. It does well against a high wall.

C. burkwoodii has flowers of crimson. C. scoparius (The Common Broom) in its form Cornish Cream,

has flowers of a colour which its name well describes. Dorothy Walpole is a rich dark red. C. kewensis is low growing and sulphur-flowered. C. atropurpureus has deep purple flowers in May. All the Brooms, once planted, strongly dislike being moved.

Above *Pampas Grass, Cortaderia argentea, holds its handsome heads up in the second half of summer till the first frosts*

Opposite *Crocosmia masonorum, with orange, montbretia-like flowers*

D

Dahlia (*Compositae*) Some connoisseurs may sniff at the dahlia, but no plant offers such a generous range of colours, and so many flowers for so long – from July till the first frosts. Some of the best from the point of view of habit, foliage, richness of colour and character, are the large flowered maroon Adolph Mayer, the mauve Lavender Perfection and the purple Town Topic. Of the smaller flowered decorative dahlias the favourite pink flowered Gerrie Hoek

is still outstanding – as is the pale gold Glorie Van Heemstede and the orange Prairie Fire.

The cactus and pompon type of dahlia are not perhaps to be considered as flowers of the first choice – nor are the collarettes – but the new Elstead strains provide attractive flower and leaf colour for the gardener who would plan his borders with an eye for originality. And those two old favourites, the deep purple white tipped Deuil du Roi Albert, and red

Below *Dahlias make a bonfire of burning colours from July until the first frosts*
Opposite left *Late summer colour in the border provided by yellow dahlias and tall pink Michaelmas Daisy, Festival, with the lower growing Jenny in front. The close planting of dahlias with michaelmas daisies is one of the most effective combinations of the late summer, early autumn border*
Opposite right *No plant family has such a range of colour as the dahlia.*

flowered winey-leaved Bishop of Llandaff, are two dahlias without which any garden would be the poorer.

Daphne (*Thymelaeaceae*) There are three daphnes which should be in every garden. D. Cneorum, miniature with pink flowers; D. Mezereum with strongly fragrant deep red flowers, and the May flowering pale pink D. burkwoodii, Somerset. This is perhaps the most refined Daphne.

Datura (*Solanaceae*) Daturas, in tubs or boxes, lend an exotic and very special air to any terrace, but have to be wintered in the greenhouse. D. suaveolens, The Angel's Trumpet, is the most beautiful white, scented datura. D. sanguinea has orange flowers.

Davidia (*Cornaceae*) Abbé David (1820–1900) sent back many plants and trees from China during his time there as a missionary, but none more beautiful than Davidia involucrata,

the Dove, or more prosaically, Handkerchief Tree, called after the striking white leaf bracts which surround its inconspicuous flowers in May. Davidia will thrive in any good soil, but is slow to flower. It is quite hardy but does not like to be in too dry a position.

Delphinium (*Ranunculaceae*) It is

difficult to think of the delphinium as being a relation of the butter-cup, but they belong to the same family. Of the many splendid border delphiniums Anne Page, the black-bee'd Harvest Moon, the lilac-mauve Lady Dorothy, rich purple-blue Sir Neville Pearson and the fine new white Mollie Hanson are five fine flowers. More unusual is the Belladonna Delphinium Ruysii, Pink Sensation, the first pure pink worth growing, the giant flowered Pacific Strains, and the exquisite Blue Butterfly which flowers its first year from seed and grows no more than 12 inches high. All delphiniums respond to a rich diet.

Desmodium (*Leguminoseae*) This is a plant which came to Europe in the year of Queen Victoria's accession. Its arching branches, weighed down with mauve pea flowers in late summer, make it the ideal plant for the top of a hot bank, or low wall. Also known as lespedeza. Its odd colloquial name is Tick Trefoil.

Dianthus (*Caryophyllaceae*) Carnations or dianthus take their name from the Greek: Dios, a God, and anthos, a flower, and there are few of the genus which do not live up to their name. Though there is no place in this book for the greenhouse varieties of carnation, such as the marvellously opulent Malmaisons, there are several rock garden and border varieties which well deserve a mention. The mat-forming pink flowered Dianthus arvernensis, erinaceus and La Bourbrille, are all attractive plants for paving, or for gritty pockets in the rock garden. D. deltoides Steriker has flowers which are a rich crimson.

For the border there are several fascinating hybrids such as the chocolate flowered French Lace, the raspberry coloured Jonathan and the pale mauve-lavender Lady. Best of all, and taking the place in the garden once held by Mrs Sinkins, is the pure white, strongly fragrant Swan Lake.

Allwood is a famous name in the

Opposite A beautiful tree for gardeners with acid soil. Davidia involucrata, the Dove, or more prosaically Handkerchief tree. Its large white bracts, hanging from inconspicuous flowers, are unusually attractive. It was named for the Abbé David (1826–1900) who sent back many excellent plants from China in the last century, among them some of the best buddleias, such as Buddleia magnifica with violet purple flowers
Below One of the glories of the summer border is delphiniums, with flowers in a dozen shades of blue, white and even pink. All delphiniums thrive on a rich diet

Opposite *Delphiniums and Campanula persicifolia Blue Belle, reflect the steely colouring of the branches of Cedrus atlantica glauca, the Blue Cedar* Right *Informal paving set about with pots of petunias and tufts of dianthus and iris*

Below *Foxgloves, Digitalis purpurea, are happiest growing in shaded woodland, where they are generous seeders. The new Excelsior hybrids have fuller flower heads in pink, deep rose, and pale yellow, as well as the usual white and purple*

carnation world, and one of the most attractive of all pinks was raised by Montagu Allwood. It is called Loveliness and its unique shredded petals give it an airy lacy quality all of its own.

Dicentra (*Papaveraceae*) The Bleeding Heart, D. spectabilis, has deeply cut glaucous leaves and attractive, elegantly arching stems of curiously shaped rosy-pink flowers. It should be given a position which is sheltered from spring frosts. Valuable for its unique habit and its ability to grow in shade.

Dictamnus (*Rutaceae*) The 'Burning Bush' has flowers of rosy-red, and aromatic foliage. It has been growing in European gardens since the reign of Queen Elizabeth. Dictamnus has a curious combustible quality, hence its popular name; it will burst into quick flame if, on a warm still evening, a match is held to its leaves and stem, the plant being quite unharmed by this odd manifestation. D. Fraxinella is the variety to grow.

Digitalis (*Scrophulariaceae*) Foxgloves are among the best of plants for naturalizing in lightly shaded woodland or semi-sunless borders. The new Excelsior strains with flowers borne all round the stem, instead of only on

Jean Jacques Rousseau described carnations as 'fit fare for Phoebus' horses' and no flower is more strongly scented
Above *Pinks (Dianthus) Mrs Sinkins lay a perfumed carpet under a row of old apple trees at Cranborne Manor in Dorset*

Left *Pinks make neat cushions of silver foliage surmounted by white, crimson-centred flowers with picotee petals*

one side, are a sensational improvement on the type. D. lutea is a worthwhile perennial foxglove, with yellow or white flowers.

Doronicum (*Compositae*) The Leopard's Banes show their golden daisy flowers early in the year. Spring Beauty is a good new variety. Though easy-going they prefer a damp situation.

Dracaena (*Liliaceae*) Dracaenas will grow well in protected gardens in the south and strike an exotic note in any border in which they are planted. D.

Draco is the Dragon Tree, one of the longest lived plants in nature, and a native of the Canary Islands.

Dracocephalum (*Labiatae*) The Dragon Flower, or sometimes Obedient Plant, is an addition to any border, with its lilac flowers which are shown at their best in partial shade. The leaves and flowers of the Obedient Plant have a curious characteristic, hence its pseudonym, of remaining in any position into which they are moved. D. Ruyschianum is the best variety.

Above *Dianthus barbatus. In the foreground the old favourite auricula-eyed variety, with flowers of white and a crimson centre*

Right *The seldom grown Dictamnus Fraxinella purpureus, dittany or Burning Bush. Its leaves and stem exhale an inflammable oil which, if a match is applied, will momentarily ignite, leaving the plant quite unharmed*

E

Eccremocarpus (*Bignoniaceae*) Eccremocarpus scaber is a showy climbing plant for a warm south wall, covered with a mass of tubular orange flowers in late summer. It should be raised from seed and planted out in May. Except in very sheltered gardens it will be cut down to the root every autumn but usually comes again in spring.

Echinops (*Compositae*) The Globe Thistles are the hardiest of perennials, and thrive in any sunny, well-drained border. Taplow Blue shows round heads of metallic blue in July and is as good as any.

Echium (*Boraginaceae*) The giant blue echiums of Southern and Mediterranean gardens are not for colder climates – but one annual echium – Blue Bedder – is an admirable plant and, if planted *in situ* in April and thinned out later, will flower from July till autumn. There are Vipers Bugloss in shades of pink, mauve and white, as well as blue.

Elaeagnus (*Elaeagnaceae*) The Elaeagnus are a useful, workaday lot, but the evergreen E. ebbingei is an excelleng hedge making plant for seaside gardeners. E. pungens aureovariegata – though far from rare, has as brilliant a foliage of green and gold as any evergreen, and E. p. variegata has leaves splashed with cream.

Epimedium (*Berberidaceae*) All epimediums are useful plants to grow in shade where their leaves make attractive ground cover. E. grandiflorum Rose Queen, with evergreen foliage and rose-pink flowers is a particularly good one. Warleyense, with orange flowers and coppery foliage is another. They prefer woodland soil.

Opposite *In a garden of rare trees in Hampshire, the spectacular Chilean Fire Bush, Embothrium coccineum shows its brilliant flowers in May. The Fire Bush was introduced to Western gardens by William Lobb in 1846. It likes an acid soil and a mild climate, as does the tree beyond, the yellow leaved maple, Acer cappadocicum*

Below *Erica Tetralix Williamsiana and Erica cinerea rubens keep a bank free of weeds, while the slim outline of Juniperus communis hibernica provides an exclamation mark*

Eremurus (*Liliaceae*) Eremurus or Fox Tail Lilies, are among the noblest of the lily family, and make spires of pale flowers – in white, cream or yellow in summer. E. Bungei is one of the most imposing. Highdown Gold has particularly lucent flowers. They do well in a limey soil.

Erica (*Ericaceae*) Of the taller ericas, Erica arborea alpina, the Tree Heath is the best and the most hardy. Its foliage is a brighter green than that of the more usually planted E. arborea, and its white flowers are more sweetly scented. A short list of the lower growing heaths, some of the most efficient ground covering plants there are, should certainly include E. carnea (pink flowers and lime tolerant). E. c. aurea (golden-leaved, pink-flowered). December Red (flowers in March), and Springwood White. Of the Erica cinereas, Golden Hue, with rich gold leaves and Purple Robe are outstanding, as is the mauve-pink Eden Valley. Other good heaths are darleyensis

Above and right *The Erica carnea group is lime tolerant and if planted in bold groups, as here, makes excellent ground cover. E. carnea has pink flowers, and is one of the best. Another good member of the group is Springwood White. In the picture above, different ericas are shown in effective contrast to a pair of upright conifers, Juniperus communis hibernica.*

Opposite *Eremurus Bungei, the noble Foxtail Lily, flowers in early summer – it appreciates sharp drainage, and a place in the sun. The recently raised Highdown Hybrids, which flower in alluring tints of coral, amber and different golds, are an improvement on the form*

Above *Eryngium alpinum Donard is a good looking Sea Holly and has flowers like those of a teasel in shades of steely blue. But the real beauty of the plant is the involucres of fine filigree that surmount its stems*

Right *The Euchryphias originate in Chile, Australia and Tasmania, and are among the most beautiful trees of late summer. All prefer acid soil and light shade. They actively dislike lime, though a British raised hybrid E. Nymansay will tolerate some chalk.*

Opposite *A bank closely covered with a natural planting of different ericas.*

Silver Beads (Silberschmelze), E. tetralix mollis, and E. vagans Holdens Pink, E. v. Lyonesse and E. v. Mrs D. F. Maxwell. It is important, when planting all the smaller heaths, to plant them in groups of at least seven or nine and to work in some peat or leaf-soil around their roots.

Erigeron (*Compositae*) The erigerons make low cushions of daisy flowers and are useful for cutting. Three good varieties are the violet Dignity, the light blue, yellow centred Sincerity, and bright pink Vanity. All should be cut down after flowering, to preserve the plant's neat form.

Eryngium (*Umbelliferae*) The Sea Hollies have decorative blue-green foliage and flower heads encircled by spiny bracts. The most beautiful to grow are alpinum, with incredibly delicate ruffs of foliage; pandanifolium, with fine exotic leaves but nondescript flowers, and the purple amethystinum. Eryngiums like light soil and full sun, and do well by the sea.

Erythrina (*Leguminosae*) The Coral Tree has an exotic appearance, and its bright red flowers fairly blaze in midsummer. E. crista galli (Cock's Comb) is the one to grow. All erythrinas need the warmest and most sheltered position possible. They are natives of Brazil.

Erythronium (*Liliaceae*) Dog's Tooth Violets are attractive plants for a damp, half shaded position, with marbled leaves which are as great an attraction as their flowers. E. Denscanis has leaves which are particoloured in purple and brown, with

Left *Erica makes the most efficient and varied of ground-coverers, as can be seen in this autumnal garden scene. The russet coloured carpet is formed of the late flowering yellow Calluna vulgaris Blazeaway, the green-leaved C. vulgaris alba and pinkish Erica vagans grandiflora. The brilliant red tree in* the background is Liquidambar styracifolia, a Sweet Gum from Eastern North America. By careful choice a show of ericas can be had all year

Above *Eucomis comosa, a bulbous plant of good outline, with columns of greenish star-shaped flowers*

73

rose coloured flowers. E. tuolumnense has bright green leaves and yellow flowers. They enjoy woodland conditions where they spread rapidly. They can be divided regularly every few years.

Escallonia (*Saxifragaceae*) Escallonias are some of the best natured of flowering evergreens and are not particular as to soil or situation. They grow well by the sea. A few of the best are C. F. Ball with crimson flowers, the long flowering Donard Brilliance, E. G. Cheeseman with bell-shaped cherry coloured flowers, and Peach Blossom, pale pink. And for gardeners in search of something out of the ordinary, there is E. illinita, with white flowers and an odd, but not unpleasant, smell of the farmyard.

Eucomis (*Liliaceae*) At the base of a warm, south facing wall, in well-drained soil is where E. comosa is most likely to succeed. Its exotic flowers are greenish-white and borne on columnar stems which can reach a foot or more in length. But it is a plant only for favoured climates.

Eucryphia (*Eucryphiaceae*) For gardens on non-calcareous soil the eucryphias are some of the most beautiful and rewarding of trees. By far the best are that great hybrid,

Above *Grasses like Eulalia sinensis variegatus associate well with water; with their roots reaching down to the moisture beneath, they quickly make graceful fountains of leaves*
Left *Euonymus fortunei gracilis has silver variegated leaves which are sometimes tinged with pink*

Opposite *Three plants for the connoisseur in one picture. Two euphorbias, the yellow E. polychroma and the orange bracted E. griffithii Fireglow, grow in the shelter of a wall curtained with pink Clematis vedrariensis rosea*

Above *One of the best of the Euphorbias. E. Wulfenii shown in juxtaposition with another plant of striking foliage Yucca Gloriosa, or Adams Needle. Beyond can be seen the bold leaves of the New Zealand Hemp— Phormium Tenax*

Nymansay (child of the delicate E. glutinosa and evergreen cordifolia, and combining the qualities of both) and the newer Rostrevor, with flowers like white anemones. But an acid soil and spadefuls of peat at planting time is essential.

Euonymus (*Celastraceae*) Euonymus alatus, with its corky bark and oriental line is spectacular, and E. fortunei gracilis, with its silver variegated foliage, and half trailing, half clinging habit is a most useful and attractive plant. E. ovatus aureus has showy leaves which are splashed with yellow, especially when planted in a sunny position.

Euphorbia (*Euphorbiaceae*) These are some of the most popular connoisseur's plants of today, and few gardens can be considered complete without at least one euphorbia. Varieties to look for are the herbaceous E. griffithii with orange-red bracts, and E. polychroma with brilliant acid-green flowers in early spring. Good shrubby euphorbias include the splendid E. Wulfenii, the best of all, the quick spreading dark green leaved E. robbiae and the trailing jade leaved E. Myrsinites. E. pulcherrima is the popular greenhouse plant poinsettia. Euphorbias are not particular as to soil and do not demand a rich diet.

Fatsia (*Araliaceae*) City gardeners, with shaded gardens and poor soil, will find a real friend in Fatsia japonica, which will grow almost anywhere. Its glossy palmate evergreen leaves are surmounted in autumn (sometimes as late as November) by umbels of cream coloured flowers.

Festuca (*Gramineae*) The blue-green Fescue grass provides a subtle touch of coloured foliage wherever it is planted. It does well in full sun and light sandy soil. To be fully effective, its tufts should be planted closely together, to form a mat. Also known as Sheeps' Fescue. Festuca Glauca is the best.

Above *Forsythia is one of the earliest shrubs to flower and its yellow blossom-hung branches make a cheerful sight in March and April. But the great value of Forsythia is the fact that if cut in tight bud and brought into a warm room its flowers will open and last in water for many days*

Foeniculum (*Umbelliferae*) Fennel makes a three-foot high feathery plant, equally useful for its graceful form, and its value in cooking. The Bronze Fennel is particularly attractive – but can seed itself about rather too freely. It thrives on chalky soil.

Forsythia (*Oleaceae*) Of the popular forsythias, three are outstandingly superior to the others. Intermedia Lynwood, primulina (with softer yellow flowers) and ovata tetragold, a smaller shrub than the type, and better suited to the smaller garden. Forsythia makes a useful cutting plant if taken after the frost has been on it. It will open quickly in a warm room.

Fothergilla (*Hamamelidaceae*) The fothergillas all have flowers like miniature bottle-bushes in spring and bright autumn colouring. They dislike heavy soil and lime. F. monticola Huntsman is the best, and it colours brilliantly.

Fremontia (*Sterculiaceae*) The quick growing Fremontia californica is a true plant for the connoisseur, but needs the warmest and most sheltered position against a wall. Its large yellow flowers are borne from early summer until October. Unfortunately, it is not a long-lived plant.

Fuchsia (*Oenotheraceae*) The hardy fuchsias make the most graceful of shrubs for town gardens. F. gracilis with pink and purple flowers is one of the hardiest. F. thompsonii, of erect growth, is one of the freest flowerers. F. versicolor has attractive variegated foliage, flushed with pink, and deep crimson and purple flowers. F. magellanica Mrs W. P. Wood has the freshest green leaves and pale pink flowers. Thalia looks different from most fuchsias, with its tubular wine coloured flowers.

Above *In a setting of different grasses, Hyacinthus candicans raises its bell towers of pure white flowers*
Left *In spring the Fritillaria imperialis shows its yellow or burnt umber flowers. The Crown Imperial, in the legend, is said to have stared too boldly at Jesus Christ and to have had to hang its flower heads, ever since, in shame*

G

Galanthus (*Amaryllidaceae*) It would be hard to find a snowdrop more desirable to naturalize in the garden than the ordinary Galanthus nivalis: but G. Elwesii is larger and the attractive green markings on its petals

more pronounced and Galanthus plicatus 'Warham' is another good form.

Galtonia (*Liliaceae*) Also known as Hyacinthus candicans, the Spire Lilies are the most useful bulbous plants, as

Above *Genista aetnensis, the elegant Mount Etna broom presents an almost Oriental outline. Its light habit of growth and airy form makes it possible to underplant it with other shrubs*

they produce their spring-like white flowers in late summer. They will naturalize well in the front of shrubberies in open sunshine, or light shade, and their flowers are slightly fragrant.

Garrya (*Garryaceae*) The male form of Garrya elliptica presents a splendid appearance in winter when its branches are hung with its characteristic long glaucous catkins. Garrya thrives by the seaside, but is tolerant of town conditions. Its swags are said to have inspired the Adam brothers. It propagates easily from cuttings in late summer, but does not like to be transplanted once it is established.

Genista (*Leguminosae*) Broom was the flower of the Plantagenets (*Plante à Genêt*) and there are several genistas which are kingly plants for the garden or shrubbery. The low growing G. hispanica, the Spanish Gorse, makes a compact dark green bush covered with golden flowers in May and June; G. Lydia shows its yellow flowers at the same time. The new G. tinctoria Royal Gold flowers a little later, as does the Mount Etna Broom, G. aethnensis, which can make an elegant tree covered with flowers in July and August. Light soil is preferable and, once planted, brooms should be left alone.

Gentiana (*Gentianaceae*) The gentians' very name is synonymous with blue. The best varieties for the discriminating gardener are G. acaulis, with brilliant blue trumpet flowers and evergreen mats of leaves; the Willow Gentian, G. asclepiadea, which is taller, with dark blue flowers on two-foot stems in late summer, and is a

Above *A corner of a border in high summer, in which roses and the blue-mauve flowers of Galega officinalis mingle their different scents.*
Left *'The hardy geraniums or Crane's bills make first class groundcover and some flower throughout the summer'. Geranium armenum has crimson, black centred flowers and makes a handsome mound of leaf and flowers in high summer*
Opposite *Ivy-leaved geraniums are the plant par excellence, as seen here, for growing in an old stone vase*

particularly good plant for naturalizing in the front of the shrub-border; the eye-catching, free flowering, but lime-hating, hybrid, Macaulayi, which flowers in September; and G. septemfida, good natured and generous in flower. G. sino-ornata grows well in soil rich in leaf mould and can flower till Christmas. The best loved gentian of all, G. verna, flowers, as its name implies, in spring.

Geranium (*Geraniaceae*) The hardy geraniums or Crane's Bills make first class ground cover and some flower throughout the summer. Some of the best are G. armenum with crimson, black centred flowers in July; G. Endressii Major Johnson's Form with larger flowers; macrorrhizum Ingwersens Variety which bears its pink flowers throughout the season, and G. lancastriense with attractive silky leaves and flesh coloured flowers. They will do well in ordinary well drained soil.

Gunnera (*Haloragidaceae*) Gunnera is the most imposing of all plants for the waterside, with its striking, giant-sized leaves. As it comes from Brazil, gunnera needs some winter protection, such as a covering of its own dead leaves. G. manicata is the best variety. They take a little time to establish.

H

Hedera (*Araliaceae*) There are several ivies of great distinction, Hedera colchica variegata is the best of all large leaved golden ivies. H. Helix Cavendishii has silvery leaves, but is a slow grower. H. cristata has unusual fringed leaves, while H. tricolor has leaves edged with white and pink. H. Buttercup is a rich yellow. Though ivies will grow almost anywhere some soil preparation at planting time yields good results. They all revel in full sun.

Helianthus (*Compositae*) The annual sunflower is surely one of the noblest of flowers, rarity or not. And there are perennial helianthus which are almost as effective, such as the opulent double Soleil d'Or and the very imposing Monarch.

Helichrysum (*Compositae*) Two helichrysums that are well worth growing are the strongly aromatic Curry Plant, H. serotinum, and the more delicate rosmarinifolium (also known as Ozothamnus rosmarinifolius) with showy pink bead-like buds opening to creamy flowers. This needs the protection of a wall in northern gardens. All helichrysum will put up with a poorish soil.

Helleborus (*Ranunculaceae*) Most hellebores grow happily in shade, and are endearing in the way they are among the very first garden plants to flower in January and February. The Christmas Rose (H. niger) and the Lenten Rose (H. viridis) sometimes even flower before the old year is out. H. foetidus has striking foliage, but of

Opposite *Blue Hydrangea hortensis in the garden of Smedmore Manor in Dorset. Hydrangeas vary in colour according to the soil in which they are planted : blue on acid soil, or pink when the soil is alkaline : to the left, the red spikes of Polygonum amplexicaule* Above *Of the many hebes with interesting leaves, the silver Hebe pageana, is one of the most attractive* Right *Twin close-clipped plants of helichrysum and lavender make perfumed cushions by steps of brick and stone. Helcihrysum serotinum is an unusual silver plant. Its foliage wafts about a pleasing scent of curry*

all hellebores, H. corsicus is the most spectacular, bearing its jade-green flower heads over well-sculptured foliage. It prefers some sun. All hellebores respond to some compost or well rotted manure at planting time.

Hemerocallis (*Liliaceae*) Recently these have been much developed and improved, and there are now Day Lilies to be had in colours unknown fifty years ago. A few of the best and most brightly coloured are the rose Pink Damask, the vermilion Rajah, the lemon-yellow Vespers, the dark brown Bagette and the almost purple Morocco Beauty. One of the beauties of hemerocallis is its graceful luminous spring foliage. They prefer a moist situation and like to grow by water.

Heracleum (*Umbelliferae*) The Giant Cow Parsleys present a superb architectural outline, but should only be grown in the wilder parts of the garden, as they are prolific seeders and can become a nuisance. Their huge forked leaves are most impressive, and their soaring stems terminating in vast umbels of cream coloured flowers are magnificent. For bigger, better leaves – and fewer unwanted seedlings – the flower heads should be cut down as soon as they start to fade. Heracleum Mantegazzianum is the one to look for.

Heucherella (*Saxifragaceae*) This is a cross between heuchera (called after the German botanist Johann Heucher) and tiarella. Bridget Bloom, with neat rosettes of dark leaves and long-lasting sprays of light pink flowers is the variety to look for. Heucherella will do well in sun or half shade and enjoys a mulch of dead leaves.

Above *Hemerocallis, or Day Lilies delight in growing by water, as these, on the bank of a lily-padded lake Hemerocallis have been immensely improved by hybridization in the last few years and are now to be had in different shades of pink, amber and maroon as well as the accustomed orange and yellow*
Left *Helichrysum angustifeltum delights in poor soil, full sun and sharp drainage*

Above *Helleborus niger, the Christmas Rose if given some protection, will flower in mid-winter. Helleborus orientalis, shown here, the Lenten Rose, flowers in spring in shades of purple or white*

Above right *The soaring outline of Heracleum Mantegazzianum, the Giant Hemlock, or cow-parsley, in a garden which might be in Kyoto, but is actually in Berkshire. Though magnificent to look at, the heracleums are prolific seeders, and best relegated to the wilder parts of the garden, and away from small gardens altogether*

Right *Unusual plants to find on a roof top garden: a Weeping Willow, Salix babylonica, and (inspite of the comments above) the giant hemlock, Heracleum Mantegazzianum*

Hibiscus (*Malvaceae*) The shrubby mallows are very useful, colourful plants for gardeners on chalk. Hibiscus syriacus Blue Bird, Duc de Brabant (double red), Hamabo (white with a crimson patch), and Woodbridge (rose-pink) are four of the best. They flower at a useful time: late summer.

Hippophae (*Elaeagnaceae*) Hippophae rhamnoides, the Sea Buckthorn, has cheerful silver foliage and a mass of orange berries which are too bitter for the hungriest bird to eat. Plants of different sexes, one male to six females – should be planted near enough to each other to make pollenization possible. Hippophae does well by the sea, on light sandy soil.

Hosta (*Liliaceae*) Of all plants for the city gardener, hostas are the most useful, as they will grow in deep shade and poor soil, though, naturally, they respond gratefully if the ground in which they are to grow is to some extent prepared.

Some of the best hostas are the magnificent H. Sieboldiana, H. Fortunei alba picta with leaves splashed with yellow, H. lancifolia with narrower green leaves and, best of all, H. crispula with leaves piped with white. Recently in Northern Ireland, I saw a new hosta with pure gold leaves grown from seed from Japan, which soon should be in commerce and is a sensational plant. The leaves of hostas are always more interesting than the flowers. They can be divided in early spring, when the new leaf spikes are just visible.

Opposite Honeysuckle curtaining a wall by a gate in a Chinese Chippendale design. Three of the best are Lonicera belgica – Early Dutch, with red and yellow flowers, the almost evergreen L. Halliana, and L. serotina

Above right Hosta Sieboldiana is one of the most beautiful of the Plantain Lilies. Its leaves are glaucous blue and great groundcoverers. On the right are the white and green dappled leaves of Scrophularia nodosa variegata

Below right Humulus scandens aureus, the Golden Hop, shows brilliant yellow leaves

Above *Hydrangeas will grow happily in pots, tubs, or as here, an old lead tank, if watered regularly. Their name, hydrangea, is formed of two Greek words, hydor, water and aggeion, a receptacle*

Left *All hydrangeas prefer light shade, and the large velvet-leaved Hydrangea Sargentiana especially appreciates the protection offered by overhanging trees. Its flowers are white and born in spreading heads of florets. H. Sargentiana was named after the distinguished founder of the Arnold Arboretum in Massachusetts, Charles Sargent (1841–1927)*

Opposite *Hydrangea macrophylla in the foreground, and a fine specimen of the yellow-flowered Genista aethnensis beyond. The Etna Broom is a particularly useful plant, as it casts little shade, and so can be effectively underplanted*

Hydrangea (*Saxifragaceae*) Hydrangeas are all happiest with their roots in cool soil. Of the many forms available, some are outstanding plants, and should be in every garden, especially shaded ones. Of the well known Hortensia groups (H. macrophylla Hortensia) the deep red Altona, the pink (or bright blue on acid soils) Holstein, the white Madame Mouilliére and rose-pink Vicomtesse de Vibraye are all good plants.

Of the species hydrangeas, H. robusta and two climbing hydrangeas, H. integerrima and petiolaris are interesting. Of the attractive lace cap group, Lanarth White (particularly good in town gardens) the grandiflora form of H. paniculata, and H. quercifolia which colours well in autumn are all good. But the two best hydrangeas for any garden are surely the velvet leaved H. sargentiana and lilac flowered H. villosa.

Hypericums (*Guttiferae*) are good natured about soil, and their golden flowers are a joy in July and August. But there are so many that it is important to plant only the best varieties. These should certainly include the shade tolerant Androsaemum with flowers that are followed by spectacular seed-vessels, H. patulum Hidcote with the largest flowers of all; the good cushion-forming olympicum, H. Moserianum tricolor with leaves particoloured in green and pink. Perhaps the best hypericum of them all is Rowallane, named after a great garden in Northern Ireland, which can grow to a height of six feet in a sheltered position.

IJ

Iris (*Iridaceae*) There are iris in as many colours as the rainbow from which they take their name. The bearded iris are the showiest, and it would be difficult to exceed in garden value such hybrids as Golden Rajah, Blue Ensign, the chartreuse-green Cleo, pale blue Jane Phillips and flamingo-pink Party Dress. But more refined by far are the species iris. Iris such as the sky-blue winter flowering unguicularis (especially in its superba form) and I. cristata lacustris, pale blue and golden centred. I. foetidissima, a shade lover, is mainly grown for its bright autumn seeds which show up well in their bursting pods. I. Kaempferi is the Japanese iris, which loves to grow by water. Two of the loveliest, and strangest, of species iris, are I. tuberosa (or Hermodactylus tuberosus) with green and black flowers, and the exotic I. susiana which has grey petals streaked with black. But these last two plants are for the specialist gardener. All iris appreciate a dressing of lime rubble.

Jasminum (*Oleaceae*) Five desirable jasmines, other than the indispensable J. nudiflorum and J. officinale, are the larger stronger-growing officinale grandiflorum, and J. revolutum, which make elegant semi-evergreen shrubs with large yellow flowers; the delicate Primrose jasmine – J. primulinum with yellow flowers, and the strongly scented J. polyanthum which needs greenhouse protection in all but the mildest districts. The hybrid jasmine, J. stephanense, with pink flowers and of rampant growth is also worth growing. J. nudiflorum, in particular benefits from a hard pruning after flowering.

Opposite *Many coloured bearded iris at the base of a sun-baked wall. In the foreground, the golden Rajah, with the rich purple Dark Fury beyond. Tips for successful iris growing : lots of old mortar rubble, cut the leaves right back after flowering, and divide clumps every three years*

Above *Magnolias, jasmines and vines revel in the warmth of the walls of a balustraded terrace at Powis Castle, in Wales. In front are box-bordered beds of heliotrope and standard fuchsias*

Below *The Satin Iris, Sisyrinchium striatum, not only delights to grow in paving, and readily seeds itself about, but will thrive in gravel, too. Its flowers are pale yellow, with a dark eye*

K

Above *Kalmia latifolia, the Mountain Laurel or Calico Bush originates in Eastern North America. It has pink chintzy flowers*

Kalmia (*Ericaceae*) Lucky is the gardener whose garden is on the acid soil suitable for growing kalmias. All are desirable, though perhaps K. lati folia Brilliant and K. l. Clementine Churchill are two of the best. It is often thought that kalmias, like rhododendrons like some shade, but they prefer full sun, and a moist soil. Kalmias are evergreen.

Kirengeshoma (*Saxifragaceae*) This is an ideal plant to put in the front of a shrub border or in shady woodland. Its leaves resemble those of a sycamore tree, and it bears its yellow bell-flowers on ebony stems in late summer. They like moist soil and can be increased by careful division in March or early April.

Kniphofia (*Liliaceae*) Kniphofia, Tritoma or Red Hot Poker is a plant which has brightened Western gardens since the reign of Queen Anne. There are many new varieties which are an improvement on the type – Royal Standard, the pale yellow Buttercup and the golden flowered, short growing Goldelse are all good plants – while the species K. caulescens, with leaves as exotic as an agaves, is specially imposing. All kniphofias must have sharp drainage, and on heavy soil should be planted on slightly raised ground as otherwise their roots may rot.

Kolkwitzia (*Caprifoliaceae*) Kolkwitzia, the Beauty Bush so popular in American gardens, is of the easiest cultivation and not particular as to soil. Pink Cloud is a good new variety with brighter flowers than the type. Kolkwitzia benefits if all its old wood is pruned back after flowering.

Opposite *Some plants associate happily with paving – such as the Kentranthus, or Valeriana officinalis*

Above *A plant for the connoisseur from Japan is Kirengeshoma palmata, with well-sculpted leaves, and pendant pale yellow flowers on slender black stems. It prefers moist, leaf-mouldy soil and protection from full sunshine*

L

Above *Lavender, pinks and mat-forming plants in a paved corner of the great Yorkshire garden at Newby Hall*

Opposite *Lavender and santolina set in squares of brick make a fragrant carpet in a garden in France. Box contributes a subtle smell of its own*

Lamium (*Labiatae*) The Dead-nettles are all great weed suppressors – though L. galeobdolon, which has silver variegated leaves, is almost too rampant for most gardens. More restrained are L. maculatum with mauve or pale pink flowers – or L. maculatum aureum, an attractive slower growing form, with pale gold leaves. Their popular name is Archangel.

Lathyrus (*Leguminosae*) The Everlasting Pea has grown in Western gardens for centuries. The usual magenta-purple flowered variety is not perhaps a plant for the specialist, but L. rubellum with rosy-pink flowers,

and the new White Pearl are attractive climbers. All lathyrus are deep rooting, and resent disturbance.

Lavandula (*Labiatae*) There are very few lavenders which can be compared to the two most popular varieties – Lavandula officinalis, the old English lavender, and L. vera, the Dutch lavender with slightly greyer leaves. However, Folgate is considered by experts to be a better plant than the popular Munstead strain, and Hidcote is a specially rich purple. London Pink is an attractive pink-flowered form. All lavenders should be pruned back after flowering.

Lavatera (*Malvaceae*) The Tree Mallows, especially Lavatera Olbia with its many rose coloured flowers and downy, hand-shaped leaves, make handsome shrubs, and will thrive on chalk and by the sea. L. maritima has bold white flowers. Of the annual mallows, Pink Domino and White Lady are outstanding. They flower in late summer, when colour is scarce in the garden.

Lilium (*Liliaceae*) Of this most beautiful race of flowers, there are just a few which should be in every lily-lover's garden. They have been chosen not only for their looks and scent, but also for their good nature and ease of culture.

'Wild' or species lilies Tigrinum, the Tiger Lily, regale, auratum, speciosum (Shuksan and Cinderella), umbellatum (Golden Chalice).

Hybrid lilies The Aurelian hybrids, especially Black Dragon, Green Dragon, Golden Clarion and Limelight, Imperial Crimson and Imperial Silver.

Mid-century hybrids Brandy Wine, Tabasco, Mountaineer, Prosperity, and the vivid red Enchantment.

Turks Cap Lilies Martagon alba, monadelphum, cernuum, chalcedonicum.

All lilies demand sharp drainage and like to have their heads in the sun while their roots are in the shade.

Above left *Pale yellow lily Golden Clarion and the tawnier African Queen. Both can grow to a height of five feet*

Above right *'Lilies would still be beautiful, but sad, if they did not smell' Lilium candidum, the Madonna Lily, and Lilium regale in a cottage setting*

Opposite *Sweetly scented lily Imperial Crimson is a cross between auratum and speciosum. Below and to the right, lily Imperial Silver*

Lobelia (*Campanulaceae*) Lobelias, if planted in masses and close together, as that great gardener Victoria Sackville-West advised, can be effective enough, but there are plants which are very different from those one sees all too often used as an edging, alternating with white candytuft. The perennial L. cardinalis – with brilliant red flowers and wine-dark foliage is a splendid example. L. vedrariensis has mauve flowers and green leaves, and L. syphilitica is light blue. The last three lobelias need some protection in winter.

Lonicera (*Caprifoliaceae*) Of the shrubby honeysuckles, two are particularly attractive plants. L. fragrantissima which can grow to thirteen feet and has scented cream coloured flowers in the dead of winter, and L. nitida Baggesens Gold with golden leaves and an elegant habit of growth.

Some of the best of the climbing honeysuckles are L. americana, L. etrusca superba, and L. japonica Halliana and L. periclymenum serotina, the late Dutch honeysuckle, and, almost best of all, L. tragophylla, with the largest orange-yellow flowers. It is hardy except in the coldest gardens.

Lunaria (*Cruciferae*) The annual Honesty is perhaps not worth growing except as a foliage plant in its less common variegated form; but its seed heads are useful, if dried for winter decoration.

Above right *The variegated form of Lunaria annua or Honesty, shows fresh green, cream flaked leaves*
Below right *Lunaria annua – or old-fashioned Honesty, is a plant for growing in the wilder parts of the garden*

Opposite *The exotic flowers of Lysichitum or Skunk Cabbage from America in a damp spot in a Hampshire garden. L. Americanum as shown here, is a rich yellow. L. Camtschatcense is white. Both have a most disagreeable smell*

Lupinus (*Leguminosae*) Lupins have recently lost the popularity they enjoyed some years ago. Their flowering season is short – their leaves are untidy (they should not be cut down until the autumn), and as plants they are short lived. But at their best, some of the Russell strains are lovely things. Blushing Bride, the oddly coloured Josephine, which has flowers of slatey-blue and lemon, the blue and white Lady Diana Abdy, and dusky Thundercloud are all great flowers.

The Tree Lupin, Lupinus arboreus, if naturalized in full sun will flower for months on end, and generously seed itself about; it is a plant of great character. The seldom grown L. Chamissonis is a real plant for the connoisseur. It has attractive grey foliage and mauve flowers in May.

Lychnis (*Caryophyllaceae*) There are several Rose Campions which make excellent border plants, L. Flos Jovis, in both its crimson and white flowered forms, and L. Flos Jovis (Sir John Hort's variety) which makes a smaller plant with pleasing pink flowers above silver leaves. Lychnis Haageana has red leaves and red flowers. Good drainage is important for all lychnis.

Lysichitum (*Araceae*) The Skunk Cabbages add an exotic luxurious note to any waterside planting, and delight in a damp situation and deep soil. L. camtschatcense from Siberia, is smaller, and its trumpet shaped flowers are white. As their colloquial name would imply, they have a strong, disagreeable smell.

Lysimachia (*Primulaceae*) By the water side, Lysimachia punctata presents spires of bright yellow flowers for months on end.

Left *Lupins rear their brightly coloured spires of flowers, while overhead floats a cloud of the blossom of Crambe cordifolia, which not only has spectacular flowers, but huge heart shaped leaves as well*

Above *A magnolia, feathery leaved Artemisia arborescens, and a yucca in full flower set a varied garden scene at a street corner in Kensington*

Magnolia (*Magnoliaceae*) All magnolias like good soil, shelter from spring frosts, and partial shade. Of all things, being woodland trees in the wild, they like a mulch of dead leaves. Some magnolias like M. Kobus, are more tolerant of lime than others.

Magnolias for the perfectionist would certainly include the splendid M. grandiflora exoniensis, the Exmouth magnolia, with huge globe-like flowers in late summer; M. parviflora, with red stamened flowers in May and June; M. soulangeana lennei, with

101

Opposite above left *Four beautiful magnolias – Magnolia stellata, the lowest growing of all magnolias. It grows slowly but has an attractively mature look from its earliest youth*
Above right *Magnolia soulangiana, one of the most perennially popular of all magnolias, has the advantage for gardeners on alkaline soil of tolerating some lime*
Below left *The rosy flowered M. soulangiana lennei is the earliest to bloom, so its flowers are liable to damage by frost*
Below right *The lily flowered M. liliflora nigra has dark purple flowers, and is a hearty grower*
Right *One of the best, and newest of the mahonias is 'Charity' It sometimes flowers at Christmas time. Mahonias thrive on any soil, including chalk*
Below *Mahonia japonica shows handsome pinnate evergreen leaves and sweet smelling pale yellow flowers in earliest spring*

purple flowers in spring; the delicate dusky flowered M. s. nigra; the sweet smelling M. stellata, a low growing magnolia, which takes many years to reach a height of five feet; and lastly, aristocrat among aristocrats, but a plant only for the patient gardener, with perfect growing conditions to offer and a gentle climate, M. Campbellii from the East Himalayas, a tree of pyramidal shape, glaucous leaves, and, after twenty years, the most beautiful rose coloured flowers in early spring.

Mahonia (*Berberidaceae*) There are several mahonias which are well worthy of garden space. Mahonia aquifolium Charity, with yellow heavily scented flowers in earliest spring, the exotic leaved M. lomariifolia, and almost best of all, the seldom grown M. Moseri, a small shrub with pink leaves in spring, changing to bright and then dark green as the season passes. All mahonias dislike being moved about.

Malva (*Malvaceae*) There are a few mallows which the discriminating gardener might well plant, especially if his garden is on chalk or very limey soil: Malva fastigiata is an imposing plant with flowers of clear pink, and the annual mallow offers flowers of different shades of crimson, white and flesh over a long period. One of their great advantages is their ability to stand up to drought.

Meconopsis (*Papaveraceae*) Of all the large poppy family, the prize must surely go to the poppies from the Himalayas, and the best of that splendid group, and the one most likely to succeed in western gardens, is Meconopsis grandis, with bright blue flowers. But these will only be borne if the plant is set in soil it likes – moist, peaty loam, and in half shade. A cross between M. betonicifolia and M. grandis, is M. sheldonii, an excellent perennial poppy, while other Himalayans of great distinction are M. Dhwojii, with yellow flowers and brown, downy spring leaves; M. Wallichii, not only blue but occasionally red and purple; and the very rare pink M. sherriffii.

Melissa (*Labiatae*) Melissa aurea is a handsome gold leaved form of the

103

ordinary balm and a striking plant for foliage effects. It makes a decorative addition to the herb border, and likes any not-too-rich soil.

Mentha (*Labiatae*) The mints not only provide an essential culinary herb but some worthwhile garden plants as well. The decorative variegated mint sometimes has whole stems of pure white leaves, M. Requienii is a prostrate carpeting plant for a damp situation with leaves which give off a pungently pleasant scent when trodden on. M. Pulegium, Pennyroyal, is another quick spreading carpeter with pale purple flowers. There are also mints scented like apple, pineapple, and Eau-

de-Cologne, which are all fascinating plants. Placed among tender things mints can become too invasive.

Mimulus (*Scrophulariacae*) Of all the Musks, M. cardinalis would seem the most desirable. Its scarlet flowers persist for months on end and its foliage remains fresh and attractive. It is an ideal plant for a damp soil, and can be increased by cuttings in spring.

Monarda (*Labiatae*) The Bergamots are fine old fashioned border flowers which should be more often planted. Two that are especially attractive are Cambridge Scarlet and the pink, purple leaved, Beauty of Cobham. They are happiest in moist soil.

Above *The Tibetan Poppies are all plants which delight in a cool root-run in soil that is full of peat. The yellow Meconopsis regia, which forms attractive furry rosettes of leaves early in the year, is one of the most impressive. To the left of the above picture is a pale flowered and as yet unnamed species of peony*

Opposite *The Tibetan blue poppies are among the most beautiful of all plants that grow in shade – but need lime-free soil, a moist, but well-drained situation, and a rich diet of peat or leaf-mould. Shown here is Meconopsis grandis, of which Branklyn is one of the best forms*

Above *A corner of an Essex garden, in which the aromatic leaves of balm (Melissa officinalis) embower a well placed seat, which in turn, is over-canopied with pale yellow banksian roses (Rosa Banksiae)*

Left *Morina longifolia, with narrow thistly leaves and delicately modelled flowers of pink and white on erect stems, comes from the Himalayas, and is a border plant which is not often planted, though quite hardy*

Morina (*Dipsaceae*) Morina has singular leaves which are spined like a thistle and long spikes of white and crimson flowers in whorls. It is an excellent subject for the front of a shrub border, and will thrive in any well-drained soil. M. longifolia is the best. Morina can be increased by seed sown in autumn or by division.

Myosotidium (*Boraginaceae*) This is a real specialist's plant, but not of the easiest culture. The Chatham Island Forget-me-not more resembles a hydrangea with its rich heads of blue flowers and corrugated leaves. It likes a cool damp position in acid soil, and a lot of water in dry weather. It responds gratefully to a dressing of fish manure. Though indelicate as to diet it is very beautiful.

Narcissus (*Amaryllidaceae*) Daffodils (Narcissus pseudo-narcissus) and what are generally called narcissus, are the naturalizing plants par excellence. They have been immensely developed in recent years and some of the new hybrids are much larger, showier and more sophisticated, if perhaps less poetically beautiful than the simple Lent Lilies from which most of them derive. Wordsworth would have been surprised by the host of new white, lemon coloured and even pink tinged daffodils which grow in modern gardens. Of these new flowers a few are outstanding: some of the best of the golden are Golden Harvest, Hunters Moon, the old favourite King Alfred and the mimosa coloured Rembrandt. Some of the most effective bi-coloured

daffodils are Ballygarvy, General Patton and the white petalled, yellow trumpeted Spring Glory. The elegant Beersheba, Cantatrice and Mrs E. Krelage have white trumpets.

Narcissus have been even more sensationally developed than daffodils. A few of the most striking are Carlton, with soft yellow perianths and finely goffered crowns, Tinker (its growers describe it as "a charming flower with a sunny disposition"), yellow and vivid red, and Chinese White, pure white; while Double Event and Golden Ducat are fully double with flowers as furbelowed as dahlias.

All these newcomers are very splendid, but perhaps for the specialist the old species narcissus have more appeal. Flowers such as the quaint Bulboco-

Above *Narcissus naturalized on a bank in a garden in Kent. The arabs have a saying that the scent of narcissus was 'food for the soul'*
dium conspicuous, (large trumpet – hardly any perianth), so suitably named the Hoop Petticoat Narcissus, the miniature N. cyclamineus, such as the twin flowered Tête à Tête, and tough little Peeping Tom. But perhaps the prettiest of the lot is Narcissus triandrus, Angel's Tears.

Nicotiana (*Solanaceae*) Tobacco plants N. affinis, offer beautiful white flowers and the most delicious fragrance, their only drawback being that they close their flowers in full sunlight. It is claimed that a new strain, Daylight, does not have this disadvantage. The recently introduced Limegreen,

a tobacco with pale green flowers, has great appeal. There are also red nicotianas, but these seem less attractive than the white and green. Nicotianas are annuals and have to be raised from seed each spring.

Nyssa (*Nyssaceae*) Nyssa sylvatica, the Tupelo, offers the brightest autumn colours imaginable and loves to be planted in acid soil, preferably near water. After all, the tree's name derives from Nyssa, a water nymph.

Nymphaea (*Nymphaeaceae*) There are several water lilies which are such outstandingly better plants than others that their names should be carefully noted. These are the splendid white Gladstoniana, the rich rose coloured Mrs Richmond, the crimson James Brydon, and Golden Sunrise. For the gardener who will take the trouble to give it the special care it needs (raising, drying and wintering indoors) N. caerulea – is a rare blue water lily.

Above '*The surface of lake, pond or pool can be embellished with water lilies far more beautiful today, than any that Monet had to paint.*' *James Brydon has flowers of rich crimson, while Mrs Richmond is rose-coloured. Gladstoniana is the largest of all white water lilies, with flowers which are sometimes ten inches across. Marliacea chromatella is a beautiful clear yellow with marbled leaves. All water lilies like full sun and water which is still*

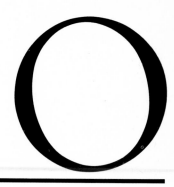

O

Ocimum (*Labiatae*) Basil is a herb which has been cultivated for use in cooking for thousands of years. It is not hardy out of doors in northern climates, but it is not difficult to grow in a pot. Its leaves are strongly aromatic. Dark Opal is a variant of the ordinary basil, with decorative purple leaves which could be used as a bedding out plant.

Oenothera (*Onagraceae*) The Evening Primrose flowers from June until autumn, and the type will seed itself generously. Two to look for are Fireworks (O. fyverkeri) and Yellow River. Missouriensis has particularly large flowers. Oenothera likes well-drained soil and will succeed in shade.

Onopordon (*Compositae*) These decorative thistles are valuable for their almost pure white, fiercely spined leaves, and noble branching habit of growth. O. arabicum can reach ten feet, O. acanthium (the Scotch Thistle) seldom tops five. Both are prolific seeders. Onopordon are biennial and should be sown in July to flower the following year.

Origanum (*Labiatae*) Sweet marjoram, Origanum Majorana, is a plant which is not only useful ground cover, but has bright golden foliage as well. It is a plant for the herb garden and for the front of any mixed border.

Othonnopsis (*Compositae*) Othonnopsis cheirifolia is not often grown, but it is a most useful plant, with glaucous strap shaped leaves which can most effectively drape a low wall or bank: but it is its leaves and unusual habit, which are its chief charm.

Above *A real plant for the connoisseur, Ozothamnus rosmarinifolium, from Tasmania, with dark green leaves and showy pink buds which open into pale cream flowers. Ozothamnus, also known as Helichrysum rosmarinifolium, is a shrub only for a mild climate. Next to it grows an elegant hydrangea which is at its best against a wall; the velvety leaved Hydrangea Sargentiana, which can grow eight foot high, and shows white flowers on slightly bristled stems*

Left *Othonnopsis cheirifolia, with jade green, spatulate leaves is seen to advantage growing over a wall*

Above *Onopordon acanthium is one of the great garden thistles, with a soaring and vigorous habit and hoary leaves which are fiercely prickled. A biennial, it comes readily from seed and is one of the most imposing plants for the back of the border*

Left *Inspired planting by the waterside in a garden in France. Among the noticeable plants are Osmunda regalis, the Royal Fern, called after Osmunder, a Scandinavian god in remote times, and Peltiphyllum peltatum, the Umbrella Plant, with its bouquets of shining leaves. Tucked away on the far left hand side of the picture can be seen the narrow leaves of Sagittaria sagittifolia*

111

PQ

Paeonia (*Ranunculaceae*) Border peonies are among the great beauties of the garden in June and there is little to choose between the many different hybrids offered. In fact a certain sameness, except in colour, among the best of border peonies, such as the pink Clara Dubois, the white Duchesse de Nemours, Lady Alexandra Duff and Sarah Bernhardt, could be considered a weakness. But this certainly cannot be said for species peonies which all have great character and differ widely in colour and form. Some of the best are P. obovata with white flowers and golden stamens, P. emodi with deeply cut foliage and papery flowers, peregrina lobata with brilliant carmine

Below *The young scarlet foliage of Pieris forrestii is at its best in early spring.*
Opposite *Peonies are the glory of the garden in June. Duchesse de Nemours (above) is creamy white. M. Jules Elio, large flowered, with petals of silvery pink. Peonies, once planted, should, if possible, never be disturbed*

flowers, and the crimson flowered lacy leafed, tenuifolia. Most beautiful of all species peonies perhaps is P. Mlokose-witchii with flowers of clear yellow.

Two beautiful peonies for the discerning gardener, and there are few more totally handsome plants, handsome in flower, in foliage and in architectural form, are the wine coloured P. Delavayi, and the yellow flowered P. lutea ludlowi. Once planted in good deep loam peonies should never be disturbed. It has been said that they actually thrive on neglect.

Papaver (*Papaveraceae*) Few of the Oriental Poppies can claim to be plants of great distinction. Their colours are brash, their foliage coarse and their flowering period short. Plant them in a border and you will have patches of ugly green from June until October. But the apricot-pink Mrs Perry or Perry's White do have attractive flowers.

For the rock garden there is P. alpinum, of which the yellow flowers and lacy silver leaves are in perfect harmony; and the so-called peony flowered annual poppies look marvellously opulent.

Passiflora (*Passifloraceae*) Passiflora caerulea is one of the most beautiful and evocative plants to be grown – and the white form, Constance Elliott, is equally fine. Hardier, however, than both of these, is P. umbilicata, with attractive small violet flowers. They are hardy in well protected gardens and have even born fruit in London.

Paulownia (*Scrophulariaceae*) Paulownia originates in China, and was introduced in the forties of the last century and named after a green-fingered Russian Grand Duchess who became Queen of Holland. It succeeds in light sandy loam and a sheltered position, but sometimes its beautiful blue foxglove-like flowers (the buds of which are formed in autumn) are cut by spring frosts. For gardeners in search of fine foliage, one way of cultivating paulownia is to prune its branches back to within a few inches of their base – the leaves it then produces are gigantic, though the flowers are lost. P. tomentosa imperialis is the kind to look for.

Peltiphyllum (*Saxifragaceae*) Peltiphyllum peltatum has large handsome leaves and rose coloured sprays of flowers – it likes a position near water where it soon makes a luxuriant clump of foliage.

Penstemon (*Scrophulariaceae*) P. barbatus Torreyi is a very special plant with bright scarlet flowers, as has P. pinifolius with leaves like heather. P. Scouleri makes a delightful neat bush, covered with large mauve flowers in early summer while P. Hartwegii Garnet, with its dark wine flowers is the hardiest of all. All penstemons like some lime in the soil.

Perilla (*Labiatae*) This is a decorative annual, worth growing for the striking effect of its dark bronze leaves, which associate well with plants of silver foliage. It must be raised under glass, and planted out in late May. Nankinensis is the one to look out for.

Perovskia (*Labiatae*) Perovskia atriplicifolia shows blue flowers on pearly white stems, and silvery foliage in July and August. It does best in a warm situation and in well-drained soil – Blue Spire is a particularly good variety with larger flowers.

Petasites (*Compositae*) The name petasites derives from the Greek word meaning a large hat and was given to the plant by Dioscorides. The only one worth growing is the giant leaved form, but it should be planted where its rampant growth will not smother more delicate plants. Its popular name is Winter Heliotrope.

Philadelphus (*Saxifragaceae*) Five of the best of all the Mock Oranges are Beauclerc, Belle Etoile (with flowers flushed purple at the centre), coronarius aureus (with golden leaves), the low growing Manteau d'Hermine, and the strongly scented Sybille. Philadelphus prefer light soil and should be pruned back after flowering.

Phlomis (*Labiatae*) The two best of the phlomis are still the well known P. fruticosa, the Jerusalem Sage, with silver velvety leaves and golden flowers each shaped like a miniature helmet, and P. italica, smaller with pinkish flowers. Phlomis like full sun and sharp drainage. In hard winters they may be

Opposite above *The low growing polygonums are effective groundcoverers and are crowned with decorative flowers for several months on end. P. affine Darjeeling Red is crimson, while the new P. Donald Loundes has red flowers and leaves which colour well in autumn. Both are great spreaders, but easily controlled*
Below left *Phlomis fruticosa, the Jerusalem sage, makes opulent mounds of grey leaves, surmounted by yellow flower heads in June*

Below right *Polygonatum multiflorum or Solomon's Seal, is a beautiful, old-fashioned plant for the north side of the wall, or for a position in woodland. It is indifferent as to soil, but prefers to be away from hot sunshine. Its small white flowers are borne on graceful arching stems*
Above *Happiest growing in the shelter of a wall, in sharply drained soil, is the late summer flowering Perowskia atriplicifolia, with blue flowers, and feathery silver foliage*

cut down but will soon come away in spring.

Phlox (*Polemoniaceae*) Phlox decussata which can be the glory of the border from July until September only do really well in a cool and damp situation. They dislike chalk.

The almost blue Caroline Van Den Berg, the delicate Mother of Pearl, Orange Perfection, and Scarlet Starfire, are all first class flowers.

For the rock garden there are several very special phlox; P. amoena variegata has variegated leaves, Blue Saucer and May Snow are two of the best of the P. Douglasii, and P. subulata Temiscaming is outstanding.

Phormium (*Liliaceae*) Phormium tenax – the New Zealand Flax, does well in all but the severest climates. It will grow in any good soil, but appreciates watering in dry spells. It looks well by water. P. variegatum has leaves that are parti-coloured in green and yellow. The rarer P. atropurpureum is much prized.

Phygelius (*Scrophulariaceae*) The Cape Figwort, if given the protection of a wall in northern gardens, will grow to a height of eight to ten feet and show its scarlet flowers from June until the first frosts. It also makes a useful border plant. P. capensis coccineus is the best variety, though it is sometimes cut to the ground in very cold winters.

Pieris (*Ericaceae*) Lucky is the gardener on acid soil for he can grow pieris, some of the most beautiful and unusual of all shrubs. Unusual because their beauty lies in their young spring foliage rather than in their flowers.

Pieris Forest Flame (a cross between P. formosa forestii Wakehurst and P. japonica) is one of the best of all pieris. Three other first class shrubs are P. japonica Bert Chandler, from Australia, with young leaves of coral pink, the hardy P. j. Christmas Cheer and P. taiwanensis with outstanding sprays of white flowers in spring, and the striking spring foliage for which all pieris are noted. They should be planted in half shade and sheltered from wind.

Piptanthus (*Leguminosae*) Piptanthus, from Nepal, grows well in any well drained soil and is tolerant of

chalk. Its yellow pea flowers show up well when the shrub is planted against a wall. P. nepalensis is the one to choose. Its handsome leaves are evergreen.

Polyanthus (*Primulaceae*) These are almost too well known to need description, but how many gardeners know that polyanthus is a man-made plant, and was first produced in the seventeenth century, as a result of crossing the ordinary primrose and cowslip? In latter years many spectacular new strains of polyanthus have been produced, some with flowers of blue and pink, colours quite new to polyanthus. The Munstead Strain, raised by Miss Gertrude Jekyll shows the most delicate range of shades of cream, yellow, orange, and white. Polyanthus like half shade, wood soil and a not too dry situation.

Polygonatum (*Liliaceae*) Solomon's Seal is a plant which is full of a very special character. Its nodding pendant green and white flower persists for months on end in early spring. Polygonatum likes a damp semi-shaded position in good loam.

Polygonum (*Polygonaceae*) There are two excellent low growing polygonums. P. affiné Darjeeling Red which has miniature spikes of crimson flowers, and the new Donald Loundes, with red flowers and foliage which colours well in autumn. In their native Himalayas, they are said to enjoy a damp situation, but in Britain any good soil seems to suit them.

Opposite above *Primula auricula have fascinating mealy flowers in such unexpected colours as grey, terra-cotta, brown and green*
Opposite below *Polyanthus grow well in deep moist soil, with leaf mould added and plenty of moisture.*
Originally a man-made cross between the wild cowslip and the primrose, the polyanthus has recently been further developed to include plants that flower in shades of blue, as well as deep rose
Right *Primula japonica has flowers in rosy-pink tiers. It likes to have its feet in water, and flower-heads in the sun*

Potentilla (*Rosaceae*) Potentillas are the best natured of plants, are lime tolerant, and though they prefer sun, most will put up with some shade. They flower for months on end. Some of the best are P. fruticosa arbuscula, which is low growing and has golden flowers; beesii with silver leaves and rich yellow flowers; the large flowered Katherine Dykes, and the white mandshurica. Tangerine has unusual orange flowers, which colour best in light shade. The tallest potentilla (six feet sometimes) is the ivory flowered Vilmoriniana.

For the rock garden P. Tonguei, with apricot flowers that are scarlet centred and the tiny P. verna nana, which makes a mat of golden flowers in April, are most desirable little plants.

Best of the herbaceous potentillas is the cherry red P. nepalensis Miss Willmott, which worthily commemorates a great gardener.

Primula (*Primulaceae*) Primulas make ideal plants for naturalizing in woodland or by the waterside. They all like a deep acid soil and above all, moisture. A few for the connoisseur are the apricot-yellow Bulleyana, the yellow scented Florindae, P. japonica Miller's Crimson, and the rose coloured rosea Delight.

But however Delightful and however Crimson there is no primula as eternally touching as the woodland primrose. "A primrose by a river's brim, a yellow primrose was to him." Him, being the dullard Peter Bell in Wordsworth's poem. But for most of us Primula vulgaris means the very spring itself.

Prunus (*Rosaceae*) How does any gardener make his pick of the immense family of prunus at his disposal? Perhaps he should look for habit of growth and autumn colouring, as much as for

Opposite *A cherry tree, with daffodils growing in rough grass – a classic example of Natural Gardening. Here Prunus sargentii subhirtella Accolade shows its hanging bouquets of pale pink flowers and coppery spring foliage, with clumps of daffodils and narcissus below*
Below *A seat of wrought iron under the flower laden branches of Philadelphus Virginal*

generosity and brilliance of flower in what can be a short flowering season. Four he would certainly choose are: P. Blireiana with its coppery leaves, double pink flowers, and handsome bearing; P. Accolade (sargentii subhirtella) for its hanging clusters of pink flowers in April; the fastigiate Amanagawa (lannesiana erecta) for its unique columnar growth; P. subhirtella, for its welcome gift of flowering in midwinter. Other prunus of great beauty are Hisakura (better than the too-often planted Kansan); the pale pink Hokusai; the elegantly shaped Shimidzu Sakura, with pure white wreaths of flowers; Shirotae, also white, but of an almost weeping habit; the dazzling Tai Haku (the Great White Cherry), and the unusual yellow Ukon, of which the leaves turn a dark red in autumn. But perhaps if there was room in the garden for only one prunus, the thoughtful gardener's choice would fall on P. sargentii, a tree of splendid form, splendid flower, and splendid autumn colour.

Pulmonaria (*Boraginaceae*) Two desirable lungworts are P. angustifolia Munstead Blue, with bright blue flowers, and P. saccharata with attractive leaves marbled with silver, and pink and blue flowers. Both like light shade and a damp situation.

Pyracantha (*Rosaceae*) The Firethorns are of the easiest cultivation, and grow in almost any kind of soil. They are excellent wall-covers in town gardens and their berries (their great beauty), are seldom eaten by birds. Some of the best are atalantioides, which needs little or no sun and berries freely; atalantioides flava, with yellow berries; the robust Lalandei, and the brilliant orange fruited Orange Glow.

Pyrus (*Rosaceae*) Of all the decorative pears by far the most desirable is the silvery Willow Leafed Pear, P. salicifolia, which is unusual in that it seems to exist only in a weeping form. All it needs is a tactful pruning to keep it in shape.

Quince – see Cydonia.

Left *One of the most graceful small trees for the smaller gardens of today is pyrus salicifolia – the Willow Leaved Pear. It is easy to plant, not being choosy about position or soil*

Above *Pulmonaria, or lungwort shows nodding blue flowers in early summer, with rough hairy leaves. It prefers a damp situation. P. saccharata has leaves which are prettily variegated*

121

R

Rhazya (*Apocynaceae*) The blue flowered rhazya (called after an Arab physician) is a herbaceous plant which is seldom planted, though it has a certain distinction. Once established it is difficult to move, as it is a deep rooter. It will prosper in any good deep loam and always arouses interest.

Rheum (*Polygonaceae*) The ornamental rhubarbs show some of the largest leaves in the garden, and their flower heads are sensational in June. R. palmatum has green leaves and deep red flowers, but R. p. atropurpureum,

with cream flowers and wine coloured foliage, is even more striking. They like to grow by, but not in, water.

Rhododendron (*Ericaceae*) For gardens on acid soil, especially if they partly consist of woodland, rhododendrons or azaleas offer a very special world of plants. Out of the thousands of species and hybrids available, a few for the connoisseur should surely include the following. Hybrid Rhododendrons: Christmas Cheer, Essex Scarlet, Gomer Waterer, Kluis Sensation, Madame Carvalho, nobleanum,

Sappho, Stella Waterer – all of the easiest culture. Others are Blue Diamond, Blue Tit, Britannia, Conroy, Crest, Doncaster, fragrantissimum (for the greenhouse), Goldsworth Yellow, Hawk, Kilimanjaro, Lady Bessborough, Lady Chamberlain, loderi King George, Mother of Pearl, Penjerrick, Polar Bear (for its July flowering), praecox, shilsonii, Tally-Ho. A few of the most rewarding species rhododendrons are: arboreum, Augustinii, bullatum, calophytum, campylocarpum, cinnabarinum, concatenans

Above left *Two great rhododendrons for gardeners on acid soil, scarlet R. shilsonii and the paler flowered R. arboreum. Both flower early in spring, while the oak branches are still bare*

Above right *Rhododendron Macabeanum from Manipur, in India, with large, pale-ribbed leaves and clustered flowers of rich yellow*
Opposite above *The lush leaves of*

Bergenia cordifolia with Rheum palmatum atropurpureum, the ornamental rhubarb
Opposite below *Rhododendrons delight in a position near water*

122

(for its curiously scented leaves), Falconeri, Griersonianum, griffithianum, Macabeanum, mucronatum, orbiculare, sinogrande, and Thomsonii.

Rhus (*Anacardiaceae*) Of the sumachs, the female form of Rhus typhina laciniata, with lacy, deeply divided leaves and fine autumn colouring is the one to look for. Rhus cotinus foliis purpureis (Notcutt's variety) is one of the very best of all red leaved shrubs. It should be pruned back each spring. Recently its name has been changed to the clumsy Cotinus Coggygria. The Venetian Sumach is one of the best of all autumn colourers.

Rodgersia (*Saxifragaceae*) The rodgersias make striking waterside plants, though they will grow well in any position that is not too dry. The pinnata hybrids with their differing leaf forms and rosy flowers, are the ones to look for.

Romneya (*Papaveraceae*) There is not much to choose between the two romneyas most often offered – R. Coulteri and R. trichocalyx – but the American hybrid White Cloud is said to be an improvement on both. Californian Tree Poppies are best grown in free standing beds, rather than at the base of warm walls, which is where they are usually planted. They do well by the sea.

Opposite *A sylvan corner by the lake in the garden at Wakehurst in Sussex, which has recently become an annexe of the world famous garden at Kew. Speciman trees planted informally reflect their greens in the water. In the background is the pale gold of Acer japonicum aureum*

Right above *Not many rhododendrons are scented – but the Loderi group is an exception, and King George is one of the best. Another late flowering and strongly scented rhododendron is Polar Bear. It has the rare advantage among rhododendrons of flowering as late as July*

Right below *The new spring growth of some of the Himalayan rhododendrons is as graceful as opening flowers*

125

Rosa (*Rosaceae*) How from the hundreds of roses available can a gardener make a choice? And yet, every experienced rose grower or knowledgeable gardener has his or her favourites. The roses recommended on these pages therefore must be accepted as the personal choice of a dedicated rose-lover, who has grown roses for many years, and has written a book on this favourite of all flowers.

Old Shrub Roses Celestial, Queen of Denmark, Louise Odier, Madame Isaac Pereire, Variegata di Bologna, Chapeau de Napoleon, Fantin Latour, Nuits de Young, William Lobb, Kazanlik, York & Lancaster, Belle de Crécy, Belle Isis, Francofurtana (Ex-Imperatrice Josephine) Tuscany Superb.

All these old roses, the very pick of the bunch, have been chosen for their beauty of flower, their scent, the harmony between their flowers and foliage and, it must be admitted, for their romantic evocative associations; for these make a great part of the charm of old roses.

Musk Roses Buff Beauty, Felicia and Penelope.

Rugosa Roses Blanc Double de Coubert, Max Graf (for its odd prostrate growth), Roseraie de L'Haye, Conrad Meyer.

Modern Shrub Roses Aloha, Ballerina, Cerise Bouquet, Clair Matin, Fritz Nobis, Fruhlingsmorgen, Kassel, Margaret Hilling, Nymphenburg, Nevada (with reservations, on account of its ungraceful habit) Raubritter (for its unique shell-like flowers).

Species Roses Persetosa (the enchanting Threepenny Bit rose), filipes Kiftsgate, Hugonis, Moyesii, rubrifolia, Wolley Dod, xanthina Canary Bird, viridiflora (for its odd green flowers – more curious than beautiful).

Floribunda Roses All Gold, Arthur Bell, Beatrice, China Town, City of Belfast, Dearest, Dimples, Elizabeth of Glamis, Galante, Honeymoon, Iceberg, Lavender Lassie, Nypels Perfection, Orangeade, Pernille Poulson, Plentiful Pink Chiffon, Pink Parfait, Rosemary, Santa Maria, Violet Carson.

Hybrid Teas Bond Street, Casanova, Eden Rose, Ena Harkness, Ernest Morse, Grand'mère Jenny, Josephine Bruce, Memoriam, Molly McGredy, Mrs Sam McGredy, Papa Meilland, Shot Silk, Speks Yellow, Superstar, Sutters Gold, Wendy Cussons, Whisky Mac.

Climbing Roses Caroline Testout, Ena Harkness, Peace, Speks Yellow, Cupid, Guinée, Mme Gregoire Staechlin, New Dawn, Pauls Lemon Pillar.

Left *Iceberg roses, with the green frothy flowers of Alchemilla mollis and the bluish leaves of Ruta graveolens in a border of mixed plants. The old brick wall behind and the gravel path in front make a classic framework*

Above *The rich crimson flowers of Ena Harkness are often at their best at their second flowering in autumn. One of the best of all hybrid tea roses* Opposite *The Floribunda rose, Plentiful, is under-planted with white and blue pansies in a garden corner which distils the very essence of a summer's day*

Above *Floribunda roses such as Pink Oberon in a border with weed suppressing Salvia officinalis and santolina*
Above left *A corner of the famous rose garden at Haddon Hall*
Left *Flowers to 'bid the rash gazer wipe his eye' are borne by floribunda roses, such as Rosemary or Frensham*

Opposite *Rosa moschata Buff Beauty has apricot coloured flowers and glossy green foliage. In front, Stachys lanata, with silver velvety leaves*

Left *Some roses are good natured enough – and strong enough growers – to give a good show of flower even if not planted in full sun. Among these are Félicitée et Perpétue, Gloire de Dijon and Madame Alfred Carrière (shown here)*

Right *Rosa moschata Felicia is one of the most scented of the Musk roses*

Below *Musk roses such as the pink budded Cornelia and cream white, lemon scented Pax are among the most strongly perfumed of all roses, and flower for several months on end*

Rosemarinus (*Labiatae*) Of the small genus of rosemaries, the most ordinary R. officinalis, is still the best. But two others which are slightly different, and have a charm of their own, are the fastigiate Miss Jessop's Variety, and the miniature, deep blue, Severn Sea. Rosemary prefers wall protection.

Rubus (*Rosaceae*) Only two of the ornamental brambles seem worthy to be included in a list of really choice plants. R. Cockburnianus (or giraldianus) for its waxy stems; R. phoenicolasius for its ruddy stems and delicious fruit. The much grown R. tridel – a cross between R. deliciosus and R. trilobus – with its short flowering period and untidy habit of growth, seems an overrated shrub.

Rudbeckia (*Compositae*) The rudbeckias are a brassy, rather common lot, but the new double Goldquelle and green coned Herbstsonne have some distinction, as has the reddish-mauve purpurea. They will succeed in any soil.

Ruta (*Rutaceae*) This is the foliage plant par excellence, and its striking blue leaves have earned it great popularity in recent years. The variegated form has an interesting appearance but is less attractive. Both should be pruned hard back in spring – but not before all danger of frost is past.

Opposite *A rose garden with a Victorian air, but planted with the best of the modern floribundas such as the creamy white Dimples and deep pink Plentiful*

Below *The incomparable modern floribunda Iceberg with ice-white, subtly scented flowers. If only lightly pruned it will soon make a graceful shrub*

S

Sagittaria (*Alismataceae*) Aquatic plants of great character, the Arrow Heads (from their arrow shaped leaves) are of the easiest culture. They are subjects rather for the stream or lakeside than for the formal pool.

Salvia (*Labiatae*) Though "Red Salvias" may have a bad name, there are enough salvias, both herbaceous and shrubby, to make them one of the great plant families.

To take the herbaceous ones first: silken leaved S. argentea: S. superba (till recently S. virgata nemorosa) S.

haematodes and the bright blue flowered S. uliginosa are fine plants, as is S. turkistanica with its hairy opalescent leaves and pungent flower spikes. The best of the shrubby salvias would include the purple form of the common sage S. purpurascens, the Painted Sage, S. tricolor with variegated leaves, and two beautiful but delicate plants S. Grahamii and S. Greggii, both with bright red flowers.

There are good annual sages too, such as the eye-catching blue S. patens, the mealy stemmed S. farinacea, Blue

Opposite above *Sanguisorba canadensis, or Burnet, shows slender spires of creamy flowers over rich tufts of deeply cut foliage. It is at its best in a cool, shaded position*

Opposite below left and right *The shrubby salvias make effective weed smotherers if clipped every spring to encourage thicker and wider growth. To the left – Purple leaved Salvias officinalis atropurpurea. To the right S. officinalis aurea, with golden leaves. S. tricolour – the Painted Sage, with leaves edged with white, and tinged with pink, is a real plant for the connoisseur*

Below left *Sambucus nigra aurea is the invaluable Golden Elder, and few trees present such bright golden leaves throughout the season.*

Below right *The silver silky haired leaves of Salvia argentea, one of the best of the great family of sages. It likes full sun and sharp drainage*

134

Bedder and the pink, white and purple leaved S. Horminum. All salvias like a place in the sun.

Sambucus (*Caprifoliaceae*) Sambucus canadensis maxima is one of the best of the elders, and has extra large flowers, with showy dark-reddish stems. Other good varieties are S. nigra aurea, one of the best of all yellow leaved shrubs; the ferny leaved S. n. laciniata and S. racemosa plumosa aurea with lacy foliage of the purest gold.

Santolina (*Compositae*) Lavender Cotton is one of the most popular of all silver leaved shrubs. S. chamaecyparissus is the most often grown and responds well to clipping. S. neapolitana is an attractive variety with lighter, airier leaves and paler flowers. S. viridis has green leaves, and is a plant for

Opposite A brick path hedged with low growing cushiony Santolina Chamaecyparissus, or Cotton Lavender, with pungently scented leaves. Above, roses such as Wedding Day and Emily Grey grow through the branches of old apple trees

Right A rose garden, with borders surrounded by low hedges of Santolina Below On top of a wall in the well drained soil it most appreciates, Cotton Lavender makes tight cushions of aromatic silver leaves if clipped well back in spring. In front hostas, especially the bold Hosta glauca, with its blue-green spreading leaves, make very effective groundcover

those who like something different. All santolinas, like so many grey leaved plants, like to be in full sun.

Schizostylis (*Iridaceae*) The finest of the Kaffir Lilies, S. coccinea grandiflora, is Mrs Hegarty, with rose coloured flowers in October. Schizostylis need a warm position at the foot of a wall, and some protection in winter. It makes a fine exclamation mark if grown in paving, and is valuable as a cut flower well into autumn.

Sedum (*Crassulaceae*) There are several far better sedums to grow than the work-a-day S. spectabile. A new form, Brilliant, has brighter flowers which last longer – and S. telephium Autumn Joy has handsome heads of long lasting crimson-bronze flowers. The red leaved form S. spectabile atropurpureum is another good sedum. They are completely soil tolerant.

Sempervivum (*Crassulaceae*) All the houseleeks have fascinating leaves, and make tight clusters in rock work or on the top of walls. They are said to ward off evil spirits. The cobweb houseleek – S. arachnoideum – has cobwebby rosettes of leaves and deep pink flowers. Granat has particularly neat dark red foliage. If they can be established on a steeply sloping roof they seem able to subsist for months without water.

Senecio (*Compositae*) Of the shrubby senecios, one is quite outstanding, and though widely planted should still find a place in every garden, Senecio Greyii. Senecio clivorum, syn. Ligularia clivorum, is a handsome plant to plant by the waterside, with spreading leaves and shaggy yellow daisy flowers, and it looks quite unlike S. Greyii.

138

Sisyrinchium (*Iridaceae*) The Satin Flowers or Rush Lilies make attractive plants to grow in paving where their Iris-like foliage makes elegant tufts, contrasting well with stone work. They are generous seeders.

Skimmia (*Rutaceae*) The useful hardworking skimmias will grow equally well on chalk or acid soils, and their bright red berries are as cheerful as their glossy leaves. Two of the best to grow are S. Foremanii, and the finest fruiter of the group, is S. reevesiana, which holds its berries through the winter. They should be planted in groups of three or five to ensure cross pollination.

Smilacina (*Liliaceae*) The False Spikenards originate in North America and Sikkim. They look well if planted in moist loam in shady woodland or in the front of shrub-borders, where their white flowers and bright green foliage are particularly fresh looking and pleasing. S. racemosa is the form usually grown.

Right *Senecio laxifolius is a shrub from New Zealand with grey felted leaves, which persist all year round, and a burst of yellow daisy flowers in summer. It is hardier than Senecio Greyii though similar. Senecio is a useful shrub for covering banks, as it is shown here*

Opposite above *Smilacina racemosa is a great addition to Western gardens. Its sweet scented white flowers are borne in feathery heads, and it flourishes in a damp, cool spot*

Opposite left *The almost vertical face of a dry wall is the position in which to plant sempervivum or House Leek — said to ward off evil spirits. Grown in this way they display their rosettes effectively, and will quickly make large clumps, needing only the minimum of moisture. To the right, a silver tuft of the Sheep's Fescue, Festuca glauca, a miniature grass which seldom grows more than nine inches high*

Opposite right *Sedum spathulifolium with mauve, frosted leaves, grows happily in the back of an old stone seat. Its flowers are yellow, and borne in high summer*

139

Above *Spiraea arguta or Bridal Wreath grows eight or ten feet if given wall protection. It is one of the airiest and freshest of wall coverers and shows sprays of white flowers in early May*

Left *The leaves of Stachys macrantha are a rich green, and adept at smothering weeds. In summer the plant is covered with full heads of purple flowers, which last well if cut*

Opposite above *An effective planting of the silver leaved Stachys lanata, the 'ever popular Lambs Lug of cottage gardens' as a close carpet between round-clipped bushes of yew, Taxus baccata*

Opposite below *Beyond a mat of stachys, Lamium maculatum lays a chequered carpet. Dead nettles are excellent weed suppressors and quick spreaders. Lamium maculatum aureum has luminous pale yellow leaves, but is of more restrained growth. Its flowers are mauve*

Solanum (*Solanaceae*) The best of all the decorative climbing potatoes is the chalk-loving, long flowering Glasnevin form of Solanum crispum. It has potato flowers which 'gleam in purple and gold'.

Spartium (*Leguminosae*) The Spanish Broom provides bright yellow flowers in late summer and succeeds in full sun. It is useful for clothing dry banks, and for planting in seaside gardens. Hard pruning (short of the old woody growth) prevents the shrub from becoming too tall and spindly.

Spiraea (*Rosaceae*) Few of the spiraeas are worthy of garden room. The most often met with, S. arguta – 'Bridal Wreath' – and S. japonica have been much planted in recent years. But S. japonica alpina is an attractive miniature shrub, and the much taller S. nipponica rotundifolia is useful in that it will grow on chalk. Its white flowers are very showy. Best of all the spiraeas is probably S. Veitchii of which the cool white flowers are specially welcome in July.

Stachys (*Labiatae*) Stachys lanata is the ever popular Lamb's Lug of cottage gardens, with leaves like silver velvet. Stachys macrantha superba is an excellent plant with dark green hirsute foliage and handsome mauve heads of flowers. Both are great ground coverers. Recently a new variety Silver Carpet has been raised which does not flower, thereby presenting a neater appearance.

Syringa (*Oleaceae*) The lilacs have wafted their scent round Western gardens for centuries, the hybrids and cultivars of the original S. vulgaris being among the best known and best loved small trees we have. A few of the very best are the mauve-pink Katherine Havemeyer, the snowy Madame Lemoine, and the violet-red, late flowering Mrs Edward Harding. These three are double. Single lilacs to look for, are the favourite Souvenir de Louis Spaeth (wine red), Marechal Foch (carmine), and the pale yellow Primrose, which first surprised gardeners in 1949.

Less well known, but equally desirable lilacs are the bone-hardy Preston Hybrids raised by Miss Isabella

Preston in Canada: the rose-pink Bellicent and pale lilac Elinor are two of the best. Two more attractive lilacs are the small leaved, low growing S. microphylla superba, which flowers on and off throughout the summer, and the miniature Korean Lilac, S. velu-tina (or palibiniana), which flowers well even when quite young. The modest size of L. velutina makes it a most useful plant for the smaller gardens of today. All syringas do well on lime soil, but appreciate regular mulching.

Good border planning should provide groups of plants of different form and leaf to give contrast. Here Stachys lanata – blue flowered Nepeta Mussinii (of which Six Hills Giant is the most imposing form) and Sedum spectabile edge a herbaceous border

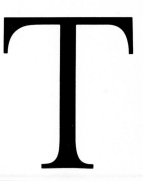

T

Tarragon (*Compositae*) There are two kinds of tarragon (Artemisia Dracunculus) French and Russian, and the former is very much the better flavoured for cooking, though sometimes difficult to find. They do well on deeply dug, well prepared soil.

Teucrium (*Labiatae*) The germanders offer silver foliage and misty, pale blue flowers, but need protection in inland gardens. By the sea and in favoured climates they flourish. T. fruticans is the best variety. In Irish gardens teucrium is sometimes clipped into a low hedge. They can be divided in spring or autumn.

Thalictrum (*Ranunculaceae*) There are at least three Meadow Rues which deserve a place in the gardens of discerning gardeners – T. aquilegifolium purpureum with fluffy heads of mauve flowers and delicate foliage, the airy T. dipterocarpum with wiry graceful stems and mauve flowers, and T. flavum with striking glaucous leaves and bright yellow flowers. They all prefer a situation which is not too dry.

Thymus (*Labiatae*) There are several thymes which have a very special charm. The golden lemon-scented citriodorus aureus, and its silver leaved form Silver Queen. T. nitidus makes a compact grey foliaged shrublet. There are three enchanting forms of the creeping T. serpyllum – the pink Annie Hall, the crimson coccineus, and the rosy-pink Chintz.

Tulips come in many different forms and in almost every colour of the rainbow; the Elizabethan herbalist John Gerard wrote of them 'Nature seems to play more with this floure than with any other that I do knowe'

143

Tiarella (*Saxifragaceae*) Tiarella wherryii is the best of the group, and presents its white foamy flowers above neat clusters of leaves. It grows best in light woodland shade.

Tigridia (*Iridaceae*) Tigridias are some of the most exotic border plants that one can grow, with spectacular but short-lived flowers. They need a sunny, well-drained position and their corms should be hung up in bags in an airy frostproof place, safe from mice, whose favourite diet they seem to be.

Tradescantia (*Commelinaceae*) An old fashioned border flower which gets its name from John Tradescant, gardener to the Stuart Kings of England. Three good forms are rubra (red), T. virginica, J. C. Weguelin (lavender-blue), and Osprey (white). They are excellent plants for town gardens.

Trillium (*Liliaceae*) The white American Wood Lily is a true connoisseur's plant, and has the rare look of all flowers with only three petals: but it must have the conditions it likes – moist, leafy soil, in woodland shade. The purple flowered variety, T. erectum, has less appeal.

Trollius (*Ranunculaceae*) Of the several trollius or Globe Flowers in cultivation, Canary Bird and the orange flowered Prichard's Giant are the ones to look for.

Tropaeolum (*Tropaeolaceae*) Two distinguished nasturtiums are the half hardy perennial T. peregrinum, the Canary Creeper, with trailing fronds of glaucous leaves and masses of yellow flowers in June; and T. speciosum which, once it is established, will drape rhododendrons or other shrubs, with festoons of scarlet flowers year after year. It likes damp soil, and some peat. It may make no sign of life for a year or so after planting, but richly rewards the patient gardener. Tropaeolum speciosum thrives in Scotland.

Tulip (*Liliaceae*) There is no better loved flower than the tulip, but there are literally so many thousand different kinds of Darwins, lily-flowered, Rembrandts, Parrots, and Bartigan tulips that choice is difficult for the least demanding of gardeners. However, twelve of the author's favourites would be Keizerskroon, Prince of Austria, Van der Neer, Purity, Rijnland, Mount Tacoma, Fantasy, Parrot Wonder, General Eisenhower, Mrs Moon, China Pink.

With the species tulips it is a different story. Some of these are very special flowers and are not as often planted as they deserve to be. Some of the most attractive are the white and crimson Lady Tulip – T. clusiana, the white and green T. tarda (though one of the earliest to flower) and the eye-catching, scarlet T. Eichleri. Loveliest of all perhaps, is T. sylvestris with several nodding pale yellow flowers on one stem.

Below *Scarlet tulip cassini in the famous bulb gardens at Springfields near Spalding*
Opposite *The garden at Abbey Leix in Ireland*

UV

Ursinia Ursinias are attractive daisy-like South African flowers which should be raised under glass and planted out later, or sown *in situ* in May. Golden Bedder is the brightest.

Valerian (*Valerianaceae*) Valerian (Kentranthus) naturalizes easily in walls. The rosy-carmine and white forms (K. macrosiphon) are more desirable plants than the more usual red. Valerian is a great seeder and flourishes on lime.

Veratrum (*Liliaceae*) In partly shaded moist positions veratrum can show leaves as spectacular as any in the garden; they are at their best in spring. Its flowers, either dark red or greenish-white, are not attractive.

Verbascum (*Scrophulariaceae*) There are many verbascums which are valuable for their soaring height and candelabra of golden (and occasionally, pink or white) flowers. The best are V. Chaixii, a ten foot biennial with splendid branching flower heads. The perennial Pink Domino, white Miss Willmott, sulphur yellow Gainsborough, or clear yellow, purple-eyed Vernale, are all good plants. For the rock garden, there is V. spinosum, a distinct and desirable shrublet seldom more than ten inches high.

Verbena (*Verbenaceae*) The most effective of all verbenas is surely V. venosa which shows its rich purple flowers for months on end in late summer. In bedding out schemes verbena associates well with geraniums: it is not quite hardy, and in cold gardens its roots should be lifted and stored for the winter.

Viburnum (*Caprifoliaceae*) The viburnums comprise some of the most valuable of all shrubs or small trees. A short list for the gardener in search of

Above *Vitis Henryana is the best of all Virginia Creepers, with more refined leaves than the type, being more elegantly veined, and colouring well in autumn*

Left *The boldly crinkled leaves of Veratrum nigrum. Veratum thrives in any rich soil and likes plenty of moisture*

Opposite *Vines offer some of the most impressive leaves of any climbing plants and there are few with finer foliage than Vitis Coignetiae, especially if the purple leaved form is planted. In the foreground are the red tubular flowers of Fuchsia Thalia*

the very best, might include V. betuli-folium, of which the branches are bowed down with scarlet fruit in autumn; the scented winter flowering bodnantense (a cross between fragrans and grandiflorum); V. Carlcephalum with its huge clusters of headily scented flowers in May; the glaucous leaved V. cylindricum; the dioecious V. Davidii, which needs to be planted with another of the opposite sex before

it produces its enchanting blue berries; the autumn flowering V. fragrans; the sweet smelling Juddii; the autumn colouring Lentago; the apricot fruited V. nudum; the impressive, shade-loving, evergreen rhytidophyllum; the Lanarth variety of V. tomentosum and the magnificent V. tomentosum Mari-esii, both of which have their white flowers strung along their horizontally growing branches in a taking and

Above *Verbascum Chaixii rears its candelabra of yellow flowers in late summer – its flannelly stems reach a height of six feet or more. A biennial, it seeds about freely. Its colloquial names are mullein, or previously, Hag's Taper*

Opposite *Phlox subulata Temiscaming laps a terrace made of old Edinburgh paving stone. Beyond the rock, Viola gracilis major*

delightful way. V. t. Mariesii is a degree less robust than the excellent Lanarth. All viburnums are happy growing on chalk or in limey soil.

Viola (*Violaceae*) A personal choice from the hundreds of kinds of violas that there are, would include V. cornuta which bears its blue flowers all summer long, gracilis Martin, deep violet, and the pale yellow V. gracilis Moonlight. Jackanapes has enchanting flowers of chocolate and yellow, with an almost human expression. Viola labradorica will grow in deep shade and has attractive dark purple leaves: it is a great spreader.

Vitis (*Vitaceae*) Of the many ornamental vines six are outstanding. V. Davidii cyanacarpa with particularly luxuriant leaves which colour well in autumn: V. vinifera Brandt which fruits well in Northern gardens, and its purple leafed form, purpurea; V. fragola with strawberry-flavoured fruit; V. Henryana (Parthenocissus Henryana), by far the most refined of the Virginia Creepers, self clinging with leaves that are veined in pink and white. And a most effective vine for any gardener is still the ever popular V. Coignetiae, especially in its purple leafed form.

Above *Leaf contrast in a well planted border – in the foreground, grey cushions of Santolina Chamaecyparissus. Behind, the towering golden flowered spires of Verbascum Chaixii, with the silver mauve flower heads of Salvia turkistanica beyond*

150

WYZ

Weigela (*Caprifoliaceae*) Three species weigelas are W. florida foliis purpureis with pink flowers and purple leaves, W. variegata with parti-coloured leaves, an excellent shrub, and the unusual yellow W. Midden-dorfiana. There are also some excellent hybrid weigelas, four of the best being the pink Abel Carriére, Bouquet Rose, the flesh-pink Heroine, and the deep crimson Eva Rathke, a late flowerer. Weigela was formerly known as dier-villa.

Wisteria (*Leguminosae*) The best of all wisterias is W. floribunda macro-botrys (multijuga) of which the falling racemes can be 3 feet long or more. Two more unusual wisterias are the white W. venusta and the almost pink W. floribunda rosea. The long shoots wisteria makes after flowering should be spurred back to two or three buds in autumn.

Yucca (*Liliaceae*) That great gardener Gertrude Jekyll called the yucca the noblest plant in the garden. Y. gloriosa (Adam's Needle) lives up to its name, though Y. filamentosa flowers more regularly. Y. variegata is a rare and tropical looking plant, with leaves striped with yellow. Yuccas should be planted in full sun, and will stand almost any amount of drought.

Zantedeschia – See Arum Lily.

Zauschneria makes a spreading carpet over rock work and brings welcome bright colour to the garden in late summer. Its orange-red flowers

Left *Wisteria curtains the corner of an old English manor in Sussex*

are tubular and borne over a long period. Z. Californica is the best.

Zinnia is one of the best loved annuals from Mexico and should be sown under glass and planted out when all chance of frost is past. There are innumerable varieties in the seedsman catalogue. Scarlet Ruffles is an eye catching newcomer.

Left *All the yuccas are plants of handsome architectural bearing, with superb heads of white bell-shaped flowers and swordlike leaves*

Right *Wisteria drapes a wall as effectively as any other climber, and its mauve, sharply scented flowers are in full beauty in early summer. Wisteria floribunda macrobotrys (multijuga) has particularly long and graceful racemes*
Below *Arum lilies – or zantedeschia – will grow well if planted by the waterside, or better still, actually in shallow water*

PLANTING GUIDE

It is useful to know the predelictions – and capabilities of different plants, for if you do right by them, they will do right by you. If you have an ugly wall to cover the right plant will quickly oblige, and be happy doing it. If your garden is shady there are plants which

Architectural Form

Acanthus
Achillea
Aegle
Agapanthus
Allium
Angelica
Bocconia
Cortaderia
Crambe
Cynara
Datura
Dicentra
Dracaena
Eremurus
Eryngium
Eucomis
Euphorbia
Foeniculum
Garrya
Heracleum
Lavatera
Morina
Myosotidium
Onopordon
Phormium
Verbascum
Yucca

Foliage

Artemisia
Atriplex
Ballota
Berberis
Bocconia
Brassica
Bupleurum
Cineraria Maritima
Davidia
Eleagnus
Euonymus
Hippophae
Lunaria
Mahonia
Perilla
Petasites
Phlomis
Pieris
Rheum
Rhus
Ruta
Salvia
Santolina
Sedum
Senecio
Skimmia
Teucrium

Groundcover

Ajuga
Alchemilla
Anaphalis
Erica
Geranium
Lamium
Polygonum
Stachys

Lime or Chalk Soil

Acer
Berberis
Buddleia
Ceanothus
Cistus
Cotoneaster
Eleagnus
Euonymus

Forsythia
Hebe
Hibiscus
Malus
Peonies
Philadelphus
Populus
Potentilla
Rosemary
Sambucus
Syringa (Lilac)
Viburnums
Weigela
Yucca

Naturalizing

Acer
Anemone
Camassia
Chionodoxa
Colchicum
Cornus
Crocus
Cyclamen
Eucryphia
Fothergilla
Galanthus
Galtonia
Genista
Gentiana

will be pleased to grow in it, and grow well. If it is on lime or chalk, do not despair, this tabulated guide, though far from comprehensive, may be a help.

Kalmia
Magnolia
Narcissus
Paulownia
Polyanthus
Primula
Prunus
Rhododendron
Smilacina
Spartium
Syringa
Tiarella
Trillium
Viburnum

Paving

Acaena
Alyssum
Arenaria
Campanula
Dianthus
Sempervivum
Thyme

Scent

Boronia
Buddleia
Daphne
Lavender
Lilium
Lonicera
Melissa
Mint
Monarda
Nicotiana
Ocimum
Origanum
Philadelphus
Rosa
Rosmarinus
Tarragon
Verbena

Shade

Aconitum
Aquilegia
Arundinaria
Bergenia
Cimicifuga
Dicentra
Digitalis
Epimedium
Fatsia
Fuchsia

Garrya
Hellebore
Hosta
Hydrangea
Kirengeshoma
Meconopsis
Pulmonaria
Tiarella
Trillium
Veratrum
Verbascum
Viola

Walls

Actinidia
Aristolochia
Caesalpinia
Camellia
Campsis
Carpenteria
Ceanothus
Choisya
Cistus
Clematis
Clianthus
Cobaea
Convolvulus
Cotoneaster
Crinum
Cydonia
Desmodium

Eccremocarpus
Fremontia
Hedera
Helichrysum
Jasmine
Othonnopsis
Passiflora
Phygelius
Piptanthus
Sisryinchium
Solanum
Tropaeolum
Valerian (Kentranthus)
Vitis
Wisteria

Waterside

Arum
Astilbe
Caltha
Doronicum
Gunnera
Hemerocallis
Lysichitum
Lysimachia
Mimulus
Nymphaea
Nyssa
Peltiphyllum
Rodgersia
Sagittaria
Spiraea
Trollius

Page numbers in italics refer to illustrations

159